Sole distributors:
Travis & Emery,
17 Cecil Court,
London, WC2N 4EZ,
United Kingdom.
(+44) 20 7 459 2129.
sales@travis-and-emery.com

the great dictators

evgeny mravinsky
artur rodzinski
sergiu celibidache

discographies
compiled by john hunt

contents

The Great Dictators
Published by John Hunt.
Designed by Richard Chluparty
© 1999 John Hunt
reprinted 2009
ISBN 978-1-901395-98-3

Acknowledgement: these publications have
been made possible by contributions or by
advance 3-volume subscriptions from

Masakasu Abe	Richard Ames
Stefano Angeloni	Stathis Arfanis
Yoshihiro Asada	Jack Atkinson
E. C. Blake	Andreas Brandmair
Peter Buescher	Eduardo Chibas
Siam Chowkwanyun	Robert Christoforides
Robert Dandois	F. De Vilder
Richard Dennis	John Derry
Hans-Peter Ebner	Henry Fogel
Peter Fu	Nobuo Fukumoto
Peter Fulop	James Giles
Jens Golumbus	Jean-Pierre Goossens
Johann Gratz	A. G. Greenburgh
Peter Hamann	James Hansford
Michael Harris	Tadashi Hasegawa
Naoya Hirabayashi	Don Hodgman
Martin Holland	John T. Hughes
Bodo Igesz	Richard Igler
Andrew Keener	Koji Kinoshita
Detlef Kissmann	Bent Klovborg
Kathryn Lanford	John Larsen
Ernst Lumpe	Elisabeth Legge-Schwarzkopf DBE
John Mallinson	Carlo Marinelli
Ryosuke Masuda	Finn Moeller Larsen
Jean-Michel Molkhou	Philip Moores
Bruce Morrison	W. Moyle
Alan Newcombe	Hugh Palmer
Jim Parsons	Laurence Pateman
James Pearson	Johann Christian Petersen
Tully Potter	Patrick Russell
Yves Saillard	Jorge Monteiro dos Santos
Neville Sumpter	Ian Sutcliffe
Yoshihiko Suzuki	Michael Tanner
H. A. Van Dijk	Mario Vicentini
Hiromitsu Wada	Urs Weber
Michael Wierer	Nigel Wood
G. Wright	Ken Wyman

Introduction

There is a theory nowadays, in our age of so-called equality, that one must be nice to people in order to get the best from them. Whether this applies in the world of practising musicians is called into doubt by the case of one of Europe's major orchestras: some years ago they appointed a chief conductor who was happy to play football with them in their spare time - the artistic results of their professional collaboration, on the other hand, have been meagre, compared that is to this particular institution's past history of excellence and integrity.

The music-making documented in the pages of these discographies is the result of a sterner relationship between conductor and musicians. Evgeny Mravinsky's iron grip on the men of the Leningrad orchestra over a period of fifty years is not only well-known but also more than fully justified by the recorded results: technique verging on perfection is placed under this conductor's firm guidance entirely at the service of the music's true expression. Passion is at its starkest by virtue of the complete absence of indulgence or of any form of exaggeration.

In contrast the high artistic demands of Artur Rodzinski and Sergiu Celibidache resulted in them both leading a more peripatetic career style as those demands repeatedly foundered against the smaller egos of the orchestras they battled with in turn. Rodzinski embarked upon one musical directorship after another in major American centres until he finally capitulated and, partly for health reasons, spent a more conciliatory indian summer with several European orchestras: indeed former members of our Royal Philharmonic Orchestra recollect that their Westminster recording sessions with Rodzinski (they played under the pseudonym of Philharmonic Symphony Orchestra of London, for contractual reasons) passed off in a mood of unalloyed affability. Not so Celibidache ! Following his being passed over in favour of Herbert von Karajan for the Berlin Philharmonic conductorship, the Rumanian spent much of his subsequent career demonstrating how second-league radio orchestras could perform at a technical level equal to the very best. Celibidache was not always thanked for the achievement, and reading between the lines it emerges that his final years with the Munich Philharmonic were not entirely harmonious.

The ultimate irony for a conductor like Celibidache, who rejected the entire recording process and its results, is that he spent so much time in the employ of broadcasting institutions who he must have known were in the business of preserving and disseminating the work of their own orchestras. Although much of the work has already infiltrated the collector's market in the form of pirate editions, Deutsche Grammophon is, as I write, announcing a definitive edition of Celibidache's recordings both from his Stuttgart years and with other institutions. I predict that Italy's RAI will not lag far behind in capitalising on this legacy of inspirational excellence.

My basis for starting work on the discography of Rodzinski was initial research by Michael Gray; in the case of Mravinsky I found the 1990 publication by the Japanese Mravinsky Society (Kenzo Amoh, Frank Forman and Hiroshi Hashizume) of the greatest help; and for Celibidache I was guided by Bruce Morrison to the Website of Tatsuro Ouchi.

Although in the past my discographies have attempted to embrace even Japanese catalogue numbers, the profligity of these (constant re-packaging and re-numbering of material already in their catalogues) renders this a herculean task from which I have shied away. Suffice it to say that there can be assumed to be multiple Japanese editions of most of the output of the major Western record companies. In the case of Mravinsky, Japanese JVC/Victor were the first to re-issue much of the material for CD, and I have mentioned this as a footnote in most cases.

evgeny mravinsky

1903-1988

discography compiled by john hunt

Deutsche
Grammophon
Gesellschaft

LENINGRAD PHILHARMONIC
ORCHESTRA

⁘⁘⁘

SERGEI RACHMANINOV

Symphony No. 2 in E minor, op. 27
Conductor: Kurt Sanderling
33 = LPM 18327

PETER TCHAIKOVSKY

"The Great Symphonies"
Symphonies Nos. 4, 5 and 6
Conductors: Evgeni Mravinsky · Kurt Sanderling
33 = LPM 18332/34
available separately

⁘⁘⁘

DEUTSCHE GRAMMOPHON (GREAT BRITAIN) LTD
12/13 Rathbone Place, Oxford Street, London W. 1.
Telephone: Langham 8156/7/8/9

JOHANN SEBASTIAN BACH (1685-1750)

orchestral suite no 2

leningrad	leningrad po	cd: russian disc RDCD 11167
21 november		also issued by king in japan
1961		

BELA BARTOK (1881-1945)

music for strings, percussion and celesta

moscow
28 february
1965
	leningrad po	lp: melodiya CM 02859-02860
		lp: emi ASD 2964
		lp: eurodisc MK 85194/KK 85194/
		    XDK 28578
		cd: olympia OCD 223/OCD 5002
		cd: zyx music ZYX 460702
		cd: documents LV 917
		cd: rca/bmg 74321 251972/
		    74321 251892
		also issued by shinsekai and
		and victor in japan

prague 24 may 1967	leningrad po	cd: praga PR 254047
leningrad 12 october 1970	leningrad po	cd: russian disc RDCD 11167 also issued by king in japan

LUDWIG VAN BEETHOVEN (1770-1827)

symphony no 1

leningrad 28 january 1982	leningrad po	cd: erato 2292 457592/2292 457632 cd: leningrad masters LM 1318 cd: audiophile classics 101.505 also issued by victor in japan; audiophile classics incorrectly dated 1983

symphony no 3 "eroica"

bergen 24 june 1961	leningrad po	cd: arkadia CD 714/CDGI 714
leningrad 31 october 1968	leningrad po	cd: erato 2292 457592/2292 457632 also issued by victor in japan

symphony no 4

leningrad 20 april 1949	leningrad po	lp: melodiya D01466-01467/ D029691-029692 also issued on lp by shinsekai and victor in japan
prague 3 june 1955	leningrad po	cd: praga PR 250021/PR 256004 also issued by king in japan
leningrad 29 april 1973	leningrad po	lp: melodiya C10 18171-18172 cd: olympia OCD 225/OCD 5002 cd: zyx music ZYX 460332 cd: documents LV 917 cd: rca/bmg 74321 251962/ 74321 251892 also issued by victor in japan; also unpublished video recording of extracts from this performance or rehearsal
tokyo 26 may 1973	leningrad po	cd: russian disc RDCD 10901 also issued by king in japan

symphony no 5

moscow 20 february 1950	leningrad po	lp: melodiya D0416-0417/D5804-5805 lp: mk records MK 1073 cd: rca/bmg 74321 294002/ 74321 294592 also issued by victor in japan; mk and rca/bmg incorrectly dated 1949
leningrad 1971	leningrad po	lp: melodiya M90 48395-48396
leningrad 8 september 1974	leningrad po	cd: leningrad masters LM 1321 incorrectly dated 1963; also issued by victor in japan
leningrad 15 september 1974	leningrad po	cd: erato 2292 457602/2292 457632 cd: leningrad masters LM 1318 also issued by victor in japan

symphony no 6 "pastoral"

moscow 29 march 1949	leningrad po	lp: melodiya D01091-01092 lp: mk records MK 1028 lp: eurodisc XK 27933/XDK 28192 also issued by shinsekai and victor in japan
leningrad 1962	leningrad po	cd: russian disc RDCD 11159 also issued by king in japan
leningrad 17 october 1982	leningrad po	cd: erato 2292 457612/2292 457632 first movement cd: erato 2292 946822 complete symphony also issued by victor in japan

symphony no 7

moscow 16 november 1958	leningrad po	lp: melodiya D04938-04939 lp: mk records MK 1029/MK 1505 lp: saga XID 5490 lp: eurodisc XK 27994/XDK 28192 cd: saga SCD 9047 cd: palladio PD 4200 cd: rca/bmg 74321 294002/ 74321 294592 also issued by shinsekai in japan
leningrad 19 september 1964	leningrad po	cd: erato 2292 457602/2292 457632 cd: leningrad masters LM 1321 also issued by victor in japan

HECTOR   BERLIOZ   (1803-1869)

symphonie   fantastique

leningrad 26 february 1960	leningrad po	cd: russian disc RDCD 10906 also issued by king in japan

un   bal/symphonie   fantastique

moscow 1949	ussr state so	78: melodiya 16695-16696

JOHANNES BRAHMS (1833-1897)

symphony no 1

leningrad 20 january 1950	leningrad po	lp: melodiya D01257-01258 lp: mk records MK 1074 cd: memoria 991.006 also issued by king in japan; mk incorrectly dated 1949

symphony no 2

leningrad 29 april 1978	leningrad po	lp: melodiya C10 18153-18154 cd: memoria 991.006 cd: artists' live recordings FED 043-044 cd: rca/bmg 74321 251902/ 74321 251892 also issued by king and victor in japan; also unpublished video recording of 28 april rehearsal
vienna 12 june 1978	leningrad po	lp: melodiya C10 15687-15688 lp: emi SLS 5212 lp: eurodisc 300 668.440 cd: eurodisc 800 029.910

symphony no 3

moscow 30 november 1971	leningrad po	cd: memoria 991.006 cd: russian disc RDCD 10905 also issued by king in japan; memoria incorrectly dated 1972; russian disc also includes rehearsal extracts dated 27 november 1971
moscow 27 january 1972	leningrad po	cd: rca/bmg 74321 294012/ 74321 294592

symphony no 4

moscow 29 december 1954	ussr state so	cd: russian disc RDCD 10916 also issued by king in japan
leningrad 14 may 1961	leningrad po	cd: russian disc RDCD 10907 also issued by king in japan
leningrad 28 april 1973	leningrad po	lp: melodiya C10 17639-17640 lp: turnabout TV 34824 cd: memoria 991.006 cd: andromeda ANR 2531 cd: artists' live recordings FED 043-044 cd: rca/bmg 74321 294012/ 74321 294592 also issued by king and victor in japan; also unpublished video recording

piano concerto no 2

leningrad 27 december 1961	leningrad po richter	cd: russian disc RDCD 11158 also issued by king in japan

ANTON BRUCKNER (1824-1896)

symphony no 7

moscow 25 february 1967	ussr state so	cd: russian disc RDCD 10911 <u>also issued by king in japan</u>

symphony no 8

moscow 24 july 1959	leningrad po	lp: melodiya D06187-06190 lp: mk records MK 1030-1031/MK 210B cd: rca/bmg 74321 294022/ 74321 294592 <u>also issued by shinsekai in japan;</u> <u>rca/bmg dated 30 june 1959</u>

symphony no 9

leningrad 30 january 1980	leningrad po	lp: melodiya C10 17643-17646 lp: turnabout TV 34832 cd: olympia OCD 220/OCD 5002 cd: zyx music ZYX 460102 cd: icon 94122 cd: leningrad masters LM 1303 cd: rca/bmg 74321 251932/ 74321 251892 <u>also issued by victor in japan;</u> <u>icon incorrectly dated 1982</u>

KARL DAVIDOV (1838-1889)

cello concerto no 2

moscow	leningrad po	cd: russian disc RDCD 10914
2 may	shafran	also issued by king in japan
1949		

CLAUDE DEBUSSY (1862-1918)

la mer

leningrad	leningrad po	cd: russian disc RDCD 11159
1962		cd: leningrad masters LM 1304
		also issued by king in japan

prélude a l'apres-midi d'un faune

moscow	leningrad po	lp: melodiya CM 02864-02865
28 february		lp: eurodisc XAK 80588
1965		cd: rca/bmg 74321 251972/
		74321 251892
		also issued by shinsekai and
		victor in japan

nuages et fêtes/nocturnes

leningrad 28 december 1952	leningrad po	lp: melodiya D1705-1706/D0438-0439
leningrad 26 february 1960	leningrad po	cd: russian disc RDCD 11167 cd: leningrad masters LM 1304 also issued by king in japan

nuages/nocturnes

moscow 1952	leningrad po	cd: multisonic 310 1782

1st rhapsody for clarinet and orchestra

leningrad 1962	leningrad po krasavin	cd: russian disc RDCD 11159 cd: leningrad masters LM 1304 also issued by king in japan

ALEXANDER GLAZUNOV (1865-1936)

symphony no 4

leningrad c. 1946	leningrad po	cd: multisonic 310 2372
leningrad 2 march 1948	leningrad po	cd: rca/bmg 74321 294072/ 74321 294592
moscow 30 march 1948	ussr state so	78: melodiya 16697-16698 scherzo only
leningrad 8 february 1950	leningrad po	78: ultraphon (czechoslovakia) H 23908-23911 lp: melodiya D9229-9230/D53-54 lp: mk records MK 1077 lp: colosseum CRLP 206 also issued by victor in japan; mk incorrectly dated 1949

symphony no 5

| leningrad 28 september 1968 | leningrad po | cd: russian disc RDCD 11165 also issued by king in japan |

the seasons, ballet

leningrad 1969	leningrad po	cd: russian disc RDCD 11155 <u>also issued by king in japan</u>

raymonda, ballet suite

leningrad 28 december 1969	leningrad po	cd: erato 2292 457672/2292 457632 <u>also issued by victor in japan</u>

raymonda, intermezzo

moscow 21 february 1965	leningrad po	lp: melodiya CM 02863 lp: eurodisc XAK 80588 cd: urania US 5163 <u>also issued by shinsekai and victor in japan</u>
tokyo 26 may 1973	leningrad po	cd: russian disc RDCD 10901 <u>also issued by king in japan</u>

MIKHAIL GLINKA (1804-1857)

ruslan and lyudmila, overture

moscow 21 february 1965	leningrad po	lp: melodiya CM 02863/C10 28431 lp: eurodisc XAK 80588 cd: urania US 5162 also issued by shinsekai and victor in japan
prague 1968	leningrad po	cd: arkadia CD 713/CD 714/ CDGI 713/CDGI 714 cd: intaglio INCD 7321 intaglio incorrectly described as london 1971
leningrad 29 november 1981	leningrad po	cd: erato 2292 457672/2292 457632 cd: icon 94172 also issued by victor in japan; icon incorrectly dated 1978
leningrad 8 april 1983	leningrad po	cd: russian disc RDCD 10912 also issued by king in japan; also unpublished video recording

valse fantaisie in b minor

leningrad 1986	leningrad po	cd: multisonic 310 2692

FRANZ JOSEF HAYDN (1732-1809)

symphony no 88

leningrad 20 april 1964	leningrad po	cd: russian disc RDCD 11163 <u>also issued by king in japan</u>

symphony no 101 "clock"

moscow 20 december 1952	leningrad po	lp: melodiya D4204-4205/ D030615-030616 lp: mk records MK 1077 lp: eurodisc XK 27992/XDK 28192 <u>melodiya and mk issues incorrectly dated 1953; according to hisashi takei a recording of the symphony issued by victor in japan and zyx music (ZYX 46152) is probably not conducted by mravinsky</u>

symphony no 104 "london"

leningrad 3 october 1965	leningrad po	cd: russian disc RDCD 11163 <u>also issued by king in japan</u>

PAUL HINDEMITH (1895-1963)

die harmonie der welt

moscow	leningrad po	
26 february		lp: melodiya CM 02861-02862
1965		lp: emi ASD 2912
		lp: eurodisc KK 80587/MK 80587/
		XDK 28578
		cd: originals SH 815
		cd: rca/bmg 74321 251952/
		74321 251892
		<u>also issued by shinsekai and victor</u>
		<u>in japan; originals incorrectly dated</u>
		<u>1978</u>

ARTHUR HONEGGER (1892-1955)

symphony no 3 "liturgique"

moscow	leningrad po	
28 february		lp: melodiya CM 02858-02859
1965		lp: emi ASD 2964
		lp: eurodisc KK 85194/MK 85194/
		XDK 28578
		lp: chant du monde LDX 78465
		cd: zyx music ZYX 46156
		cd: rca/bmg 74321 251952/
		74321 251892
		<u>also issued by shinsekai and</u>
		<u>victor in japan</u>

VASILY KALINNIKOV (1866-1901)

symphony no 2

leningrad 1953	leningrad po	cd: russian disc RCDC 11155 also issued by king in japan

ARAM KHACHATURIAN (1903-1978)

piano concerto

prague 1 june 1946	czech po oborin	cd: praga PR 250017 also issued by king in japan

BORIS KLYUZNER (1909-1975)

symphony no 2

leningrad 3 march 1964	leningrad po	cd: russian disc RDCD 11162 also issued by king in japan

ANATOL LIADOV (1855-1914)

baba yaga, symphonic poem

moscow 21 april 1959	leningrad po	cd: russian disc RDCD 10900 also issued by king in japan
moscow 28 february 1965	leningrad po	lp: melodiya CM 02863-02864 lp: eurodisc XAK 80588 cd: olympia OCD 221/OCD 5002 cd: urania US 5163 vhs video: collets CML 2020 also issued by shinsekai and and victor in japan
leningrad 30 september 1966	leningrad po	cd: russian disc RDCD 10902 also issued by king in japan
tokyo 26 may 1973	leningrad po	cd: russian disc RDCD 10901 also issued by king in japan

the enchanted lake, symphonic poem

leningrad 30 september 1966	leningrad po	cd: russian disc RDCD 10902 also issued by king in japan

FRANZ LISZT (1811-1886)

mephisto waltz

| moscow
14 february
1947 | leningrad po | lp: melodiya D09999-10000/
    D1097-1098
lp: mk records MK 1079
also issued by victor in japan |

BORIS LYATOSHINSKY (1895-1968)

symphony no 3

| leningrad
29 december
1955 | leningrad po | cd: russian disc RDCD 10902
also issued by king in japan |

FRANTISEK MICA (1694-1744)

symphony in d

| moscow
23 january
1950 | leningrad po | lp: melodiya D08518-08519 |

WOLFGANG AMADEUS MOZART (1756-1791)

symphony no 33

leningrad 2 february 1950	leningrad po	lp: melodiya D07973-07974 lp: mk records MK 1078 also issued by shinsekai in japan
london 23 september 1960	leningrad po	cd: bbc legends BBCL 40027
leningrad 25 february 1961	leningrad po	cd: russian disc RDCD 10909 also issued by king in japan
leningrad 31 march 1972	leningrad po	lp: melodiya M10 43989-43990
leningrad 24 december 1983	leningrad po	lp: melodiya C10 23719 000 cd: erato 2292 457582/2292 457632 also issued by victor in japan

symphony no 39

moscow 27 july 1947	leningrad po	lp: melodiya D08517-08518/ D851-852 lp: mk records MK 1078 mk incorrectly dated 1950

moscow
23 february
1965
	leningrad po	lp: melodiya CM 02855-02856/
		    C10 02855 000
		lp: eurodisc KK 85139/XDK 28192
		lp: ricordi OCL 16201
		cd: rca/bmg 74321 251912/
		    74321 251892
		also issued by shinsekai and
		victor in japan

leningrad 6 may 1972	leningrad po	cd: erato 2292 457582/2292 457632 also issued by victor in japan

symphony no 40

leningrad 18 april 1978	leningrad po	cd: russian disc RDCD 10901 also issued by king in japan

violin concerto no 5

vienna	leningrad po	cd: cetra CDE 1025/CDAR 2034
21 june	oistrakh	cd: stradivarius STR 10005
1956		<u>stradivarius dated 8 june 1956</u>

horn concerto no 3

leningrad	leningrad po	cd: russian disc RDCD 10909
14 may	buyanovsky	<u>also issued by king in japan</u>
1961		

sinfonia concertante for wind soloists and orchestra

leningrad	leningrad po	cd: russian disc RDCD 10909
25 november	buyanovsky,	<u>also issued by king in japan</u>
1961	nikonchuk,	
	krasavin,	
	yeremin	

don giovanni, overture

| leningrad
29 november
1968 | leningrad po | cd: russian disc RDCD 10911
<u>also issued by king in japan</u> |

le nozze di figaro, overture

| bergen
14 august
1961 | leningrad po | cd: arkadia CD 714/CDGI 714 |

| moscow
23 february
1965 | leningrad po | lp: melodiya CM 02863-02864
lp: eurodisc XAK 80588
cd: olympia OCD 223/OCD 5002
cd: artists' live recordings FED 043-044
cd: andromeda ANR 2531
cd: rca/bmg 74321 251912/
    74321 251892
<u>also issued by shinsekai and</u>
<u>victor in japan</u> |

MODEST MUSSORGSKY (1839-1881)

khovantschina, prelude

moscow 21 february 1965	leningrad po	lp: melodiya CM 02863-02864 lp: eurodisc XAK 80588 cd: olympia OCD 221/OCD 5002 cd: urania US 5162 cd: rca/bmg 74321 251912/ 74321 251892 also issued by shinsekai and victor in japan
leningrad 24 november 1982	leningrad po	cd: russian disc RDCD 10905 also issued by king in japan
leningrad 19 march 1983	leningrad po	cd: erato 2292 457672/2292 457632 cd: multisonic 310 2692 also issued by victor in japan

NIKOLAI OVSYANIKO-KULIKOVSKY (1768-1846)

symphony no 21

leningrad 16 june 1954	leningrad po	lp: melodiya D851-852/D2954-2955 lp: westminster XWN 18191 cd: rca/bmg 74321 294042/ 74321 294592

SERGEI PROKOFIEV (1891-1953)

symphony no 5

leningrad 28 september 1968	leningrad po	cd: russian disc RDCD 11165 cd: leningrad masters LM 1301 cd: czar classics 260 3012 also issued by king in japan

symphony no 6

moscow 13 december 1958	leningrad po	lp: melodiya D05016-05017 lp: mk records MK 1080 lp: artia ALP 158 lp: bruno BR 14048 cd: urania US 5163 cd: multisonic 310 1892 also issued by shinsekai and victor in japan
leningrad 21 april 1959	leningrad po	cd: russian disc RDCD 10900 also issued by king in japan
prague may 1965	leningrad po	cd: arkadia CD 713/CDGI 713 cd: praga PR 250079/PR 256004 cd: palladio PD 4200 cd: intaglio INCD 7321 intaglio incorrectly described as london 1971
leningrad 8 september 1974	leningrad po	cd: victor (japan) VICC 40148
vienna 3 june 1982	leningrad po	unpublished radio broadcast

romeo and juliet, ballet suite no 2

leningrad 24 march 1952	leningrad po	78: melodiya 22455-22467 lp: melodiya D522-523 lp: mk records MK 1076 lp: vanguard VRS 6004 lp: monarch MEL 701 lp: stradivarius STR 623 lp: chant du monde LDXA 8073 also issued by shinsekai and victor in japan
bergen 14 august 1961	leningrad po	cd: arkadia CD 713/CDGI 713
leningrad 29 june 1973	leningrad po	cd: russian disc RDCD 11180 also issued by king in japan
leningrad 30 december 1981	leningrad po	lp: melodiya C10 23719 003 lp: philips 420 4831 cd: philips 420 4832 cd: leningrad masters LM 1301 cd: czar classics 260 3012 cd: rca/bmg 74321 251942/ 74321 251892 also issued by victor in japan; philips incorrectly dated 21 december 1981
vienna 3 june 1982	leningrad po	unpublished radio broadcast
leningrad 24 november 1982	leningrad po	unpublished video recording

contents of the suite may vary in the different recordings

MAURICE   RAVEL   (1875-1937)

boléro

moscow 30 december 1952	leningrad po	78: melodiya 022864-022867 lp: melodiya D01503-01504/ D 9703-9704 lp: mk records MK 1079 cd: multisonic 310 1782
leningrad 26 february 1960	leningrad po	cd: russian disc RDCD 10906 cd: leningrad masters LM 1304 also issued by king in japan

pavane pour une infante défunte

leningrad 26 february 1960	leningrad po	cd: russian disc RDCD 10906 cd: leningrad masters LM 1304 also issued by king in japan

NIKOLAI RIMSKY-KORSAKOV (1844-1908)

legend of the invisible city of kitesh, suite arranged by sternberg

leningrad	leningrad po	cd: multisonic 310 1782
4 april		cd: rca/bmg 74321 294082/
1949		74321 294592

russian easter festival overture

leningrad	leningrad po	cd: live best classics (japan)
1975		LCB 088/LCB 144

VADIM SALMANOV (1912-1978)

symphony no 1

leningrad 20 march 1957	leningrad po	lp: melodiya C10 12977-12982

symphony no 2

leningrad 30 march 1960	leningrad po	lp: melodiya C10 12977-12982 <u>world premiere performance</u>
leningrad 1966	leningrad po	cd: russian disc RDCD 11023 <u>also issued by king in japan</u>
leningrad 4 april 1984	leningrad po	unpublished video recording

symphony no 3

leningrad 24 may 1965	leningrad po	lp: melodiya C10 12977-12982

symphony no 4

leningrad 31 january 1977	leningrad po	lp: melodiya C10 12977-12982 cd: olympia OCD 225/OCD 5002 <u>world premiere performance</u>

FRANZ SCHUBERT (1797-1828)

symphony no 8 "unfinished"

moscow 24 april 1959	ussr state so	cd: russian disc RDCD 10903 also issued by king in japan
leningrad 30 april 1978	leningrad po	lp: melodiya C10 22371 007 cd: audiophile classics 101.508 cd: zyx music ZYX 461282 cd: artists' live recordings FED 043-044 cd: rca/bmg 74321 251902/ 74321 251892 also issued by victor in japan
vienna 12 june 1978	leningrad po	lp: melodiya C10 15691-15692 lp: emi SLS 5212 lp: eurodisc 300 668.440 lp: ricordi OCL 16201 also issued by victor in japan; also unpublished video recording
minsk 20 november 1983	leningrad po	unpublished video recording

ALEXANDER SCRIABIN (1872-1915)

poeme de l'extase

moscow 22 december 1958	leningrad po	lp: melodiya D04942-04943 cd: multisonic 310 1782 also issued by shinsekai and victor in japan
moscow 21 april 1959	leningrad po	cd: russian disc RDCD 10900 also issued by king in japan

DIMITRI SHOSTAKOVICH (1906-1975)

symphony no 5

leningrad 27 march 1938	leningrad po	78: melodiya 06820-06833 recorded 4 months after the world premiere performance by mravinsky and the leningrad philharmonic
moscow 9 july 1954	leningrad po	lp: melodiya D02283-02284 lp: mk records MK 1022 lp: vanguard VRS 6025 lp: eurodisc XDK 89519 cd: rca/bmg 74321 294042/ 74321 294592 also issued by shinsekai and victor in japan; rca/bmg dated 2 april 1954
moscow 24 november 1965	leningrad po	cd: russian disc RDCD 10910 also issued by king in japan
prague 26 may 1967	leningrad po	cd: arkadia CD 714/CDGI 714 cd: praga PR 250085 arkadia dated may 1968
tokyo 26 may 1973	leningrad po	cd: russian disc RDCD 11023 cd: audiophile classics 101.503 rehearsal and performance of section from first movement vhs video: teldec 4509 957103 section from final movement also issued on laserdisc in japan

shostakovich symphony no 5/concluded

leningrad 29 june 1973	leningrad po	cd: russian disc RDCD 11180 <u>also issued by king in japan;</u> <u>also unpublished video recording</u>
vienna 12-13 june 1978	leningrad po	lp: melodiya C10 15321-15322 lp: emi SLS 5212 lp: eurodisc 300 668.440 cd: eurodisc 880 028.910 <u>also issued by victor in japan</u>
moscow 18 november 1982	leningrad po	unpublished radio broadcast
minsk 20 november 1983	leningrad po	laserdisc issue in japan only
leningrad 4 april 1984	leningrad po	cd: erato 2292 457522/2292 457632 cd: leningrad masters LM 1311 <u>also issued by victor in japan; also</u> <u>unpublished video recording of</u> <u>rehearsal extract</u>

symphony no 6

moscow 4 november 1946	leningrad po	lp: melodiya D2488-2489/ D030616-030617 lp: chant du monde LDXA 8267 also issued by shinsekai and victor in japan
prague 21 may 1955	leningrad po	cd: praga PR 254017
moscow 21 february 1965	leningrad po	lp: melodiya CM 02857-02858/ C10 12955-12956 lp: emi ASD 2805 lp: eurodisc KK 80568 lp: angel 40202 cd: zyx music ZYX 461562/461572 excerpts lp: melodiya C60 12957-12958 also issued by shinsekai and victor in japan
moscow 27 january 1972	leningrad po	cd: russian disc RDCD 10910 cd: icon 94042 cd: rca/bmg 74321 251982/ 74321 251892 also issued by king in japan

symphony no 7 "leningrad"

moscow 26 february 1953	leningrad po	lp: melodiya D01380-01383/ 　D033449-033452 lp: vanguard VRS 6030-6031 cd: rca/bmg 74321 294052/ 　74321 294592 also issued by shinsekai and victor in japan

symphony no 8

leningrad 2 june 1947	leningrad po	lp: melodiya D03620-03621/ 　D032639-032640 lp: mk records MK 1081/MK 219B lp: eurodisc XDK 89519 cd: rca/bmg 74321 294062/ 　74321 294592 also issued by shinsekai and victor in japan
london 23 september 1960	leningrad po	lp: melodiya D09615-095617 lp: mk records DO 9615 lp: bruno BR 14064 cd: bbc legends BBCL 40027 it has recently been suggested that lp editions contain a different concert performance of the work
leningrad 27 march 1982	leningrad po	unpublished video recording of rehearsal performance
leningrad 28 march 1982	leningrad po	cd: philips 422 4422 cd: icon 94112 cd: russian disc RDCD 10917 also issued by king in japan; russian disc incorrectly dated 27 march 1982

symphony no 10

leningrad 24 april 1954	leningrad po	lp: melodiya D02243-02244/ D032508-032509 lp: mk records MK 1523 lp: concert hall CHS 1313 lp: colosseum CRLP 173 lp: classics club X 1018 lp: chant du monde LDX(A) 8113 lp: saga XID 5228 cd: saga SCD 3366/SCD 9017 allegro lp: melodiya C10 28431-28434 also issued by shinsekai in japan; colosseum incorrectly names conductor as dimitri shostakovich
prague 3 june 1955	leningrad po	cd: praga PR 250053 also issued by king in japan
leningrad 3 march 1976	leningrad po	cd: erato 2292 457532/2292 457632 also issued by victor in japan
leningrad 31 march 1976	leningrad po	lp: melodiya M10 44371-44372 cd: leningrad masters LM 1322 cd: rca/bmg 74321 251982/ 74321 251892 also issued by victor in japan

symphony no 11 "year 1905"

leningrad 3 november 1957	leningrad po	cd: russian disc RDCD 11157 also issued by king in japan
moscow 2 february 1959	leningrad po	lp: melodiya D05555-05556/ 　　D4808-4811/D06295-06297 lp: mk records MK 1027/MK 210B cd: revelation RV 10091 also issued by sinsekai and victor in japan
prague 1967	leningrad po	cd: praga PR 254018

symphony no 12 "year 1917"

moscow 1961	leningrad po	lp: melodiya D09395-09396/ S0245-0246 lp: mk records MK 1580 lp: emi ASD 2598/SLS 5025 lp: angel 40128 lp: bruno BR 14065 lp: eurodisc KK 74485/MK 74485 lp: chant du monde LDX 78465 cd: urania US 5162 also issued by shinsekai and victor in japan; recorded shortly after world premiere performance by mravinsky and the leningrad philharmonic
prague 6 january 1962	leningrad po	cd: praga PR 254017
leningrad 29 april 1984	leningrad po	cd: russian disc RDCD 10912 also issued by king in japan
leningrad 30 april 1984	leningrad po	cd: erato 2292 457542/2292 457632 also issued by victor in japan; also unpublished video recording

symphony no 15

leningrad   leningrad po   lp: melodiya M10 43653-43654
5-6   also issued by victor
may
1972

leningrad   leningrad po   lp: melodiya C10 19299-19300
26 may   cd: olympia OCD 224/OCD 5002
1976   cd: zyx music ZYX 460572/ZYX 460702
                                          cd: rca/bmg 74321 251922/
                                              74321 251892
                                          also issued by victor in japan

violin concerto no 1

leningrad
30 november
1956
	leningrad po
	oistrakh
		lp: melodiya D03658-03659/
		    D5540-5541/D033451-033452
		lp: parlophone PMB 1014
		lp: telefunken TW 30213
		lp: eurodisc ZK 79829/XGK 89511/
		    XPK 88665
		lp: bruno BR 14017
		lp: monitor MC 2014/MCS 2014
		lp: period SHO 342/SHOST 342
		lp: emi SLS 5058
		lp: chant du monde LD 8186/
		    LDXS 8342
		cd: chant du monde LDC 278882
		cd: monitor MCD 62014
		cd: urania ULS 5171
		cd: rca/bmg GD 69084
		also issued by shinsekai and nippon
		columbia in japan; recorded one year
		after world premiere performance
		by oistrakh, mravinsky and the
		leningrad philharmonic

prague may 1957	czech po oistrakh	cd: praga PR 250052
leningrad date not confirmed	leningrad po ricci	cd: opus 111 EPR 95030

song of the forests, oratorio

moscow 1949	ussr state so and chorus kiltchevski, petrov	78: melodiya 019191-019199 lp: melodiya D0486-0487 lp: vanguard VRS 422 lp: chant du monde LDA 8000/ LDX 8000/LDX 8387/LDXA 8000 excerpts 78: chant du monde PA 5077 also issued by shinsekai and victor in japan; recorded shortly after world premiere performance by mravinsky and ussr state symphony orchestra

festival overture

leningrad 21 april 1955	leningrad po	cd: russian disc RDCD 10902 also issued by king in japan

JEAN SIBELIUS (1865-1957)

symphony no 7

moscow 23 february 1965	leningrad po	lp: melodiya CM 02860-02861 lp: emi ASD 2805 lp: eurodisc KK 80586 lp: angel 40202 cd: olympia OCD 223/OCD 5002 cd: zyx music ZYX 460712 cd: rca/bmg 74321 251912/ 74321 251892 also issued by shinsekai and victor in japan

the swan of tuonela

leningrad 14 may 1961	leningrad po	cd: russian disc RDCD 10907 also issued by king in japan
moscow 23 february 1965	leningrad po	lp: melodiya CM 02864-02865 lp: emi ASD 2805 lp: eurodisc XAK 80588/XBK 86851 cd: olympia OCD 223/OCD 5002 cd: rca/bmg 74321 251912/ 74321 251892 also issued by shinsekai and victor in japan

RICHARD STRAUSS (1864-1949)

eine alpensinfonie

leningrad   leningrad po   lp: melodiya C10 17781-17782
21 april   cd: olympia OCD 222/OCD 5002
1962   cd: rca/bmg 74321 294032/
                                              74321 294592
                                         also issued by victor in japan

horn concerto no 1

leningrad   leningrad po   cd: russian disc RDCD 11163
24 april   buyanovsky   cd: rca/bmg 74321 294032/
1964   74321 294592
                                         also issued by king in japan; russian
                                         disc incorrectly dated 1967

IGOR STRAVINSKY (1882-1972)

agon

leningrad 29-30 october 1965	leningrad po	lp: melodiya M10 43989-43990 cd: olympia OCD 224/OCD 5002 cd: rca/bmg 74321 251922/ 74321 251892 29 october performance was the ussr premiere of the work

apollon musagete

moscow 26 february 1965	leningrad po	lp: melodiya C10 02855-02856 lp: eurodisc KK 85193 lp: angel 40402 cd: rca/bmg 74321 251972/ 74321 251592 also issued by shinsekai and victor in japan; recorded 4 months after ussr premiere by mravinsky and the leningrad philharmonic
leningrad 27 january 1972	leningrad po	cd: russian disc RDCD 10908 also issued by king in japan

le baiser de la fée

| leningrad 1983 | leningrad po | cd: russian disc RDCD 11160 also issued by king in japan |

l'oiseau de feu, ballet suite

| leningrad 1960 | leningrad po | cd: leningrad masters LM 1313 cd: icon 94012 |

petrushka

| leningrad 1946 | leningrad po | cd: multisonic 310 1892 |
| leningrad 24 october 1964 | leningrad po | cd: russian disc RDCD 11162 cd: icon 94012 also issued by king in japan |

PIOTR TCHAIKOVSKY (1840-1893)

symphony no 4

leningrad 17 may 1957	leningrad po	lp: melodiya D04098-04099 lp: monitor MLP 8001 lp: telefunken LT 6623 cd: revelation RV 10055 cd: rca/bmg 74321 294072/ 74321 294592 also issued by shinsekai and victor in japan; revelation and rca/bmg dated 8 april 1957
prague 1957	czech po	vhs video: teldec 4509 957103 section from final movement only
moscow 24 april 1959	ussr state so	cd: russian disc RDCD 10903 also issued by king in japan
wembley 14-15 september 1960	leningrad po	lp: dg LPM 18 657/SLPM 138 657/ 2535 235/2538 178/2720 065/ 2721 085/2726 040/ 2727 012/413 5411 lp: melodiya D8107-8108/S0147-0148/ C10 16537-16538/M10 43653 000 lp: chant du monde LDXP 8235/ LDXSP 1530 cd: dg 419 9452 also issued on lp by philips

symphony no 5

moscow date not confirmed	moscow ro	78: melodiya 16417-16418 third movement only
leningrad 1947-1948	leningrad po	78: ultraphon (czechoslovakia) H 23865-23870 lp: melodiya D011-012 lp: mk records MK 1019 also issued by shinsekai and victor in japan
leningrad 19 january 1949	leningrad po	cd: russian disc RDCD 10914 also issued by king in japan; russian states that recording made in moscow
vienna june 1956	leningrad po	lp: dg LPM 18 333 lp: decca (usa) DL 9884/DXE 142 lp: eterna 820 022 cd: dg 447 4232

vienna
9-10
november
1960
	leningrad po	lp: dg LPM 18 658/SLPM 138 658/
		    2535 236/2538 179/2720 065/
		    2721 085/2726 040/
		    2727 012/413 5411
		lp: melodiya D08115-08116/
		    S0449-0450/C10 16537-16538
		cd: dg 419 7452/439 4342
		also issued on lp by philips

tchaikovsky symphony no 5/concluded

bergen 14 august 1961	leningrad po	cd: arkadia CD 714/CDGI 714
leningrad 29 april 1973	leningrad po	lp: melodiya C10 17319-17320 cd: olympia OCD 221/OCD 5002 cd: andromeda ANR 2523 cd: documents LV 917 cd: rca/bmg 74321 251962/ 74321 251892 <u>also issued by victor in japan</u>
vienna 13 june 1978	leningrad po	lp: melodiya C10 15571-15572 lp: emi SLS 5212 lp: eurodisc 300 668.440 <u>also issued by victor in japan</u>
leningrad october- november 1982	leningrad po	laserdisc issue in japan of rehearsal extracts, including complete performance of last movement
moscow 18 november 1982	leningrad po	cd: russian disc RDCD 10908 <u>also issued by king in japan</u>
leningrad 11 march 1983	leningrad po	cd: erato 2292 457552/2292 457632 cd: icon 94042 cd: audiophile classics 105.111 cd: russian disc RDCD 10905 <u>sections from first and final movements</u> vhs video: teldec 4509 957103 <u>russian disc also contains rehearsal</u> <u>extracts</u>
leningrad 29 april 1984	leningrad po	unpublished video recording

symphony no 6 "pathétique"

moscow 1949	ussr state so	78: melodiya 016903-016914
leningrad 25 march 1949	leningrad po	lp: melodiya D0237-0238 lp: kingsway (usa) KL 302 lp: colosseum CRLP 213 lp: chant du monde LDXA 8039 cd: rca/bmg 74321 294082/ 74321 294592 also issued by shinsekai and victor in japan
vienna june 1956	leningrad po	lp: dg LPM 18 334 lp: decca (usa) DL 9885/DXE 142 lp: eterna 820 023 cd: dg 447 4232

vienna 7-9 november 1960	leningrad po	lp: dg LPM 18 659/SLPM 138 659/
		    2535 237/2538 180/2720 065/
		    2721 085/2726 040/
		    2727 012/413 5411
		lp: melodiya D08263-08264/
		    S0451-0452/C10 00451-00452
		cd: dg 419 7452
		also issued on lp by philips

leningrad 24 december 1983	leningrad po	cd: erato 2292 457562/2292 457632 cd: originals SH 815 also issued by victor in japan

violin concerto

leningrad date not confirmed	leningrad po oistrakh	cd: palladio PD 4200 also issued by multisonic

piano concerto no 1

leningrad 3 march 1953	leningrad po serebriyakov	lp: melodiya D01400-01401 lp: westminster XWN 18179 lp: saga XID 5043/FID 2021 cd: multisonic 310.3522 also issued by shinsekai in japan

leningrad
24 july
1959
	leningrad po
	richter
		lp: melodiya D05468-05469/
		    CM 02013-02014/C10 02013 000
		lp: mk records MK 1001/MK 1501
		lp: vox S 16620/STPL 51337/VSPS 2
		lp: bruno BR 41007
		lp: period 1163/SHO 341/SHOST 2341
		lp: westminster WGM 8228
		lp: everest SDBR 3345
		lp: discocorp RR 516
		lp: hall of fame HOF 505/HOFS 505
		lp: murray hill M 2958/S 2959
		lp: eurodisc KK 74589/ZK 77211/
		    XA 87692/XGK 89831
		lp: eterna 826 152
		lp: cetra BU 15
		lp: vedette VSC 4007
		lp: supermajestic BBH 16220
		lp: ember ECL 9001
		lp: chant du monde LDX 8268/MV 226/
		    LDX 78711/LDXS 8268/OPM 2013
		cd: urania ULS 5175
		cd: chant du monde LDC 278.848
		cd: rca/bmg GD 69048/74321 170832
		also issued by shinsekai, victor, fontana
		and nippon columbia in japan, and
		possibly in some overseas territories
		by emi; some lp issues incorrectly
		name conductor and orchestra as
		kondrashin and moscow philharmonic

leningrad 29-30 march 1971	leningrad po gilels	cd: russian disc RDCD 11170 cd: leningrad masters LM 1306 cd: czar classics 260.3082 also issued by king in japan

capriccio italien

moscow
23 february
1950
	leningrad po	lp: melodiya D0239-0240/
		    D026214-026215
		lp: mk records MK 1021
		lp: eurodisc KK 85193/XAK 88797
		cd: zyx music ZYX 461452
		cd: russian disc RDCD 15003
		cd: rca/bmg 74321 294092/
		    74321 294592
		also issued by king, shinsekai
		and victor in japan

francesca da rimini

moscow 1940	moscow po	78: melodiya 010273-010278 78: ultraphon (czechoslovakia) H 23899-23901
leningrad 10 march 1948	leningrad po	cd: russian disc RDCD 15003 cd: rca/bmg 74321 294092/ 74321 294592 also issued by king in japan
leningrad 19 march 1983	leningrad po	cd: erato 2292 457572/2292 457632 cd: icon 94102 cd: russian disc RDCD 1160 also issued by king and victor in japan

serenade for strings

leningrad march 1949	leningrad po	cd: russian disc RDCD 15003 cd: revelation RV 10055 cd: rca/bmg 74321 294092/ 74321 294592 also issued by king in japan; russian disc dated 1948
moscow 20 april 1949	leningrad po	lp: melodiya D026213-026214/ D389-390 lp: eurodisc XAK 88797 also issued by shinsekai and victor in japan
leningrad 1961	leningrad po	cd: russian disc RDCD 11160 also issued by king in japan

casse noisette, suite extracted by mravinsky from items not
included in the standard concert suite (départ des invités;
la bataille;   dans la pinede en hiver;   danse des flocons de neige;
la fée dragée et le prince charmant;   valse finale et apothéose)

leningrad 22 november 1946	leningrad po	lp: melodiya D03426-03427 lp: mk records MK 1075/MK 1545 <u>also issued by victor in japan</u>
leningrad 31 december 1981	leningrad po	lp: melodiya C10 23521-23522 lp: philips 420 4831 cd: philips 420 4832 cd: leningrad masters LM 1314 cd: icon 94012 cd: rca/bmg 74321 251942/ 74321 251892 cd: russian disc RDCD 10905 <u>also issued by victor in japan and on cd by zyx music; russian disc incorrectly dated november 1982</u>

marche/casse noisette

leningrad	leningrad po	78: melodiya 20421-20422/D512-513
11 march		78: ultraphon (czechoslovakia)
1948		C 23944

danse de la fée dragée et coda/casse noisette

leningrad	leningrad po	78: melodiya 20423-20424/D514-515
22 november		
1946		

danse arabe/casse noisette

leningrad	leningrad po	78: melodiya 20421-20422
11 march		
1948		

danse chinoise/casse noisette

leningrad	leningrad po	78: melodiya D512-513
11 march		
1948		

danse des mirlitons/casse noisette

leningrad	leningrad po	78: melodiya D20423-20424
11 march		
1948		

valse des fleurs/casse noisette

leningrad	leningrad po	78: melodiya D514-515
22 march		lp: melodiya D03426-03427
1948		lp: mk records MK 1075/MK 1545
		also issued by victor in japan

scene dansante/sleeping beauty

leningrad	leningrad po	78: melodiya D707-708
27 april		lp: melodiya D3424-3425
1947		lp: mk records MK 1076
		also issued by victor in japan

pas de six/sleeping beauty

leningrad	leningrad po	78: melodiya 18607-18608/D707-708
27 april		lp: melodiya D3424-3425
1947		lp: mk records MK 1076
		also issued by victor in japan

adagio from prologue/sleeping beauty

leningrad	leningrad po	78: melodiya 18534-18535/D709-710
27 april		
1947		

finale from prologue/sleeping beauty

leningrad	leningrad po	lp: melodiya D3424-3425
27 april		lp: mk records MK 1076
1947		also issued by victor in japan

valse/sleeping beauty

leningrad	leningrad po	78: melodiya D198-199
27 april		lp: melodiya D3424-3425
1947		lp: mk records MK 1076
		also issued by victor in japan

marche from act 3/sleeping beauty

leningrad   leningrad po   78: ultraphon (czechoslovakia)
27 april   H 23947
1947

rose adagio/sleeping beauty

leningrad   leningrad po   78: melodiya D709-710
27 april   lp: melodiya D3424-3425
1947   lp: mk records MK 1076
                                                 also issued by victor in japan

pas de quatre/sleeping beauty

leningrad   leningrad po   78: melodiya D711-712
27 april   lp: melodiya D3424-3425
1947   lp: mk records MK 1076
                                                 also issued by victor in japan

pas de caractere/sleeping beauty

leningrad   leningrad po   78: melodiya D711-712
27 april
1947

unspecified extracts from sleeping beauty issued on melodiya 78 discs
18523-18524 and 18525-18526

GALINA USTVOLSKAYA (born 1919)

childrens' suite

leningrad   leningrad po   lp: melodiya D04430-04431
10 april
1957

RICHARD WAGNER (1813-1883)

götterdämmerung, siegfried's funeral march

leningrad 8 december 1958	leningrad po	lp: melodiya D04943-04944 lp: mk records 1032 also issued by shinsekai in japan
leningrad 1967	leningrad po	cd: russian disc RDCD 11166 also issued by king in japan
leningrad 30-31 march 1978	leningrad po	lp: melodiya C10 17783-17784 cd: olympia OCD 222/OCD 5002 cd: erato 2292 457622/2292 457632 cd: leningrad masters LM 1315 cd: rca/bmg 74321 251992/ 74321 251892 also issued by victor in japan

lohengrin, prelude

leningrad 1967	leningrad po	cd: russian disc RDCD 11166 also issued by king in japan
leningrad 11 march 1973	leningrad po	cd: erato 2292 457622/2292 457632 cd: andromeda ANR 2523 cd: icon 94172 cd: rca/bmg 74321 251992/ 74321 251892 also issued by victor in japan; rca/bmg incorrectly dated 1978
leningrad 30-31 march 1978	leningrad po	lp: melodiya C10 17646-17647 cd: audiophile classics 101.511 also issued by victor in japan

lohengrin, act 3 prelude

moscow 23-26 february 1965	leningrad po	lp: melodiya CM 02864-02865 lp: eurodisc XAK 80588 cd: olympia OCD 224/OCD 5002 cd: andromeda ANR 2523 cd: documents LV 917 cd: rca/bmg 74321 251992/ 　　74321 251892 also issued by shinsekai and victor in japan
leningrad 1967	leningrad po	cd: russian disc RDCD 11166 also issued by king in japan
leningrad 11 march 1973	leningrad po	cd: erato 2292 457622/2292 457632 also issued by victor in japan

siegfried, forest murmurs

leningrad 1967	leningrad po	cd: russian disc RDCD 11166 also issued by king in japan
leningrad 1973	leningrad po	cd: leningrad masters LM 1315

die meistersinger von nürnberg, overture

leningrad 1967	leningrad po	cd: russian disc RDCD 11166
leningrad 29 january 1977	leningrad po	cd: erato 2292 457802/2292 457632 rehearsal performance
moscow 30 march 1978	leningrad po	cd: icon 94172
leningrad 31 january 1982	leningrad po	lp: melodiya C10 22372-22373 cd: rca/bmg 74321 251992/ 74321 251892 also issued by victor in japan

tannhäuser, overture

leningrad 8 december 1958	leningrad po	lp: melodiya D04942-04943 lp: mk records MK 1032 cd: olympia OCD 220/OCD 5002 cd: andromeda ANR 2523 cd: documents LV 917 also issued by shinsekai in japan
leningrad 1967	leningrad po	cd: russian disc RDCD 11166 also issued by king in japan
leningrad 29 january 1977	leningrad po	cd: erato 2292 457802/2292 457632 rehearsal performance
leningrad 30-31 march 1978	leningrad po	lp: melodiya C10 17646-17647 cd: rca/bmg 74321 251992/ 74321 251892 also issued by victor in japan
leningrad 31 january 1982	leningrad po	cd: erato 2292 457622/2292 457632 cd: leningrad masters LM 1315 also issued by victor in japan; all incorrectly dated

tristan und isolde, prelude and liebestod

leningrad 1967	leningrad po	cd: russian disc RDCD 11166 also issued by king in japan
leningrad 30-31 march 1978	leningrad po	lp: melodiya C10 17783-17784 cd: olympia OCD 221/OCD 5002 cd: leningrad masters LM 1315 cd: erato 2292 457622/2292 457632 cd: andromeda ANR 2523 cd: documents LV 917 cd: rca/bmg 74321 251992/ 74321 251892 also issued by victor in japan; andromeda and documents incorrectly dated 1965

die walküre, ride of the valkyries

leningrad 8 december 1958	leningrad po	lp: melodiya D04942-04943 lp: mk records MK 1032 also issued by shinsekai in japan
moscow 23 february 1965	leningrad po	cd: rca/bmg 74321 251992/ 74321 251892
leningrad 1967	leningrad po	cd: russian disc RDCD 11166 also issued by king in japan
leningrad 31 march 1978	leningrad po	cd: erato 2292 457622/2292 457632 cd: leningrad masters LM 1315 also issued by victor in japan

CARL MARIA VON WEBER (1786-1826)

aufforderung zum tanz, arranged by weingartner

leningrad 2 january 1951	leningrad po	78: melodiya 19030-19033/D145-148 lp: melodiya D029691-029692 lp: mk records MK 1079
moscow 29 december 1954	ussr state so	cd: russian disc RDCD 10916 also issued by king in japan

euryanthe, overture

moscow 29 december 1954	ussr state so	cd: russian disc RDCD 10916 also issued by king in japan
moscow 24 april 1959	ussr state so	cd: russian disc RDCD 10903 also issued by king in japan

der freischütz, overture

moscow 24 april 1959	ussr state so	cd: russian disc RDCD 10903 also issued by king in japan

oberon, overture

leningrad 2 january 1951	leningrad po	78: melodiya 018988-018989/ D143-144 lp: melodiya D029691-029692 lp: mk records MK 1079
moscow 29 december 1954	ussr state so	cd: russian disc RDCD 10916 <u>also issued by king in japan</u>
leningrad 14 may 1961	leningrad po	cd: russian disc RDCD 10907 <u>also issued by king in japan;</u> <u>also unpublished video recording</u>
leningrad 29 april 1978	leningrad po	lp: melodiya C10 22372-22373 cd: icon 94172 cd: artists' live recordings FED 043-044 cd: rca/bmg 74321 251902/ 74321 251892 <u>also issued by victor in japan</u>
vienna 12 june 1978	leningrad po	lp: melodiya C10 15691-15692 lp: emi SLS 5212 lp: eurodisc 300 668.440 <u>also issued by victor in japan</u>

Yevgeni
Mravinsky
conducts

Honoured Ensemble of the Russian Republic Leningrad Philharmonic
Symphony Orchestra

P. HINDEMITH
The Harmony of the World
symphony (1951)

Дирижирует
Евгений
Мравинский

Заслуженный коллектив Республики Симфонический оркестр Ленинградской государственной филармонии

П. ХИНДЕМИТ
Гармония мира
симфония, соч.1951г.

ROYAL FESTIVAL HALL

General Manager: T. E. BEAN, C.B.E.

Tuesday, 20th September, 1960

VICTOR HOCHHAUSER

in association with

GRANADA TV NETWORK

presents the

LENINGRAD SYMPHONY ORCHESTRA

The State Symphony Orchestra of the Leningrad Philharmonia

(Leader: ILYA SHPILBERG)

Conductor:

EUGENE MRAVINSKY

Programme

GOD SAVE THE QUEEN

SOVIET NATIONAL ANTHEM

Overture: Russlan and Ludmilla   -   -   -   *Glinka*
(1804-1857)

Symphony No. 6 in E flat, Op. 111   -   -   -   *Prokofieff*
(1891-1953)
       Allegro Moderato
       Largo
       Vivace

INTERVAL

Symphony No. 5 in E minor, Op. 64   -   -   *Tchaikovsky*
(1840-1893)
       Andante — Allegro con anima
       Andante cantabile, con alcuna licenza
       Valse: *Allegro moderato*
       Andante maestoso — Allegro vivace

ROYAL FESTIVAL HALL

General Manager: T. E. BEAN, C.B.E.

Friday, 23rd September, 1960

VICTOR HOCHHAUSER

in association with

GRANADA TV NETWORK

presents the

LENINGRAD SYMPHONY ORCHESTRA

The State Symphony Orchestra of the Leningrad Philharmonia

(Leader: ILYA SHPILBERG)

Conductor:

EUGENE MRAVINSKY

in the presence of

DMITRI SHOSTAKOVICH

Programme

GOD SAVE THE QUEEN

SOVIET NATIONAL ANTHEM

Symphony No. 33 in B flat (K.319)   -   *Mozart*

    Allegro assai
    Andante moderato
    Menuetto
    Finale — Allegro assai

INTERVAL

Symphony No. 8, Op. 65   -   -   -   *Shostakovich*

    Adagio
    March Militaire
    Allegro Non Troppo
    Passacaglia
    Largo
      Dedicated to EUGENE MRAVINSKY
      First public performance in this country

artur

rodzinski,

conducting

the cleveland orchestra

shostakovich / symphony no. 1 in f major op. 10

sibelius / symphony no. 5 in e flat major op. 82

artur rodzinski

1892-1958

discography compiled by john hunt

ISAAC ALBENIZ (1860-1909)

iberia, excerpts (el corpus en sevilla; triana), arranged by arbos

london	rpo	lp: hmv ALP 1688/ASD 281
6 may		lp: hmv (france) CTRE 6130
1958		lp: capitol G 7176/SG 7176
		lp: angel 60021
		lp: emi CFP 40261/1C 045 01657
		cd: emi CZS 568 7422

navarra, arranged by arbos

london	rpo	lp: hmv ALP 1688/ASD 281
6 may		lp: hmv (france) CTRE 6130
1958		lp: capitol G 7176/SG 7176
		lp: angel 60021
		lp: emi CFP 40261/1C 045 01657
		cd: emi CZS 568 7422

LUDWIG VAN BEETHOVEN (1770-1827)

symphony no 1

cleveland 28 december 1941	cleveland orchestra	78: columbia (usa) M 535 lp: columbia (usa) RL 3047
vienna 7-9 march 1952	niederöster- reichisches tonkünstler- orchester	lp: remington 199-156 released without rodzinski's approval and using a pseudonym

symphony no 5

new york 1944	nypso	cd: legends LGD 123
new york august 1946	nypso	video recording of first movement only for the film "carnegie hall"

walthamstow
28-30
september
1956
	rpo	lp: westminster XWN 18700/
		    WST 14001/WST 16006/WM 1031/
		    WMS 1031/LAB 7058/WGS 8123
		lp: westminster (germany) P 279
		lp: music guild MS 173
		lp: heliodor 426 001/428 009/
		    476 001
		cd: mca MCAD 29808/MCD 80096/
		    MVCW 18010
		first movement
		45: ricordi ERC 25005
		45: heliodor 466 015
		lp: westminster XWN 18738
		orchestra described for this recording
		as philharmonic symphony orchestra

symphony no 7

| new york 1946 | nypso | cd: as-disc AS 513 |

violin concerto

| new york 14 january 1945 | nypso heifetz | lp: rococo 2070 lp: discocorp RR 491 cd: as-disc AS 520 cd: legends LGD 123 cd: iron needle IN 1358 cd: music and arts CD 766 |

egmont overture

| new york 1946 | nypso | cd: as-disc AS 513 cd: legends LGD 123 |

leonore no 3 overture

| new york 1946 | nypso | cd: as-disc AS 513 |
| vienna 7-9 march 1952 | niederöster- reichisches tonkünstler- orchester | lp: remington 199-156 released without rodzinski's approval and using a pseudonym |

ALBAN BERG (1885-1935)

violin concerto

cleveland 15 december 1940	cleveland orchestra krasner	78: columbia (usa) M 465 78: columbia (australia) LOX 594-596 lp: columbia (usa) ML 4857 cd: dante LYS 146

HECTOR BERLIOZ (1803-1869)

symphonie fantastique

cleveland 12 april 1941	cleveland orchestra	78: columbia LX 25025-25030 78: columbia (usa) M 488 78: columbia (argentina) 266463-266468 lp: columbia (usa) RL 3059

GEORGES BIZET (1838-1875)

symphony in c

new york 1944	nypso	cd: as-disc AS 535 cd: radio years RY 52
new york 15 january- 23 may 1945	nypso	78: columbia (usa) M 596 78: columbia (france) LFX 870-873 lp: columbia (usa) ML 2051/RL 6629

carmen, excerpt (l'amour est un oiseau rebelle)

warsaw 1930s	orchestra werminska <u>sung in polish</u>	lp: muza XL 0112

carmen, act 3 entr'acte

new york 12 march 1945	nypso	78: columbia (usa) M 596/ 12252D/12905D

carmen, suites 1 and 2

walthamstow 2-14 october 1954	rpo	lp: westminster XWN 18230 lp: vega C30A-023 lp: heliodor 478 018 cd: mca MVCW 18004 <u>orchestra described for this recording</u> <u>as philharmonic symphony orchestra</u>

l'arlesienne, suite no 1

walthamstow	rpo	lp: westminster XWN 18230/LAB 7006
2-14		lp: westminster (germany) P 279
october		lp: vega C30A-023
1954		lp: heliodor 478 018
		lp: emi MFP 2097
		cd: mca MVCW 18004
		<u>orchestra described for this recording</u>
		<u>as philharmonic symphony orchestra</u>

l'arlesienne, suite no 2

walthamstow	rpo	lp: westminster XWN 18230/LAB 7005
2-14		lp: westminster (germany) P 279
october		lp: vega C30A-023
1954		lp: heliodor 478 018
		cd: mca MVCW 18004
		<u>orchestra described for this recording</u>
		<u>as philharmonic symphony orchestra</u>

l'arlesienne, farandole

new york	columbia so	45: columbia (usa) A 1002
15 february		45: philips NBE 11075/N409 538E/
1950		SBF 130/S313 424F
		lp: columbia (usa) ML 4311
		lp: philips SBL 5204/S04601L/
		GBL 5568/G03561L

ERNEST BLOCH (1880-1959)

schelomo for cello and orchestra

walthamstow	rpo	lp: westminster XWN 18007/
12-13	janigro	WST 14985/W 9732
october		lp: vega C30A-077
1954		orchestra described for this recording
		as philharmonic symphony orchestra

ALEXANDER BORODIN (1833-1887)

polovtsian dances

walthamstow	rpo	lp: westminster XWN 18542/
1 may		LAB 7039/WH 20095
1955		lp: vega C35S-135
		lp: ricordi MRC 5020
		cd: mca MVCW 18009
		orchestra described for this recording
		as philharmonic symphony orchestra

JOHANNES BRAHMS (1833-1897)

symphony no 1

new york 8 january 1945	nypso	78: columbia (usa) M 621 lp: columbia (usa) ML 4016/ RL 3117/P 14120 cd: dante LYS 258 incorrectly described by dante as a live recording

symphony no 2

new york 14 october 1946	nypso	78: columbia (usa) M 725 lp: columbia (usa) ML 4068/P 14136 cd: dante LYS 241 incorrectly described by dante as a live recording

violin concerto

new york 23 january 1944	nypso huberman	lp: rococo 2007

walthamstow
9-23
september
1956
	rpo
	morini
		lp: westminster XWN 18600/
		    WMS 1011/WST 14037/WG 8354/
		    WHS 20047
		lp: ricordi MRC 5043
		lp: heliodor 428 004/478 016
		lp: emi 1C 045 91171
		cd: mca UMD 80394
		orchestra described for this recording
		as philharmonic symphony orchestras

FREDERIC CHOPIN (1810-1849)

piano concerto no 1

vienna 28 june- 8 july 1954	vienna state opera orchestra badura-skoda	lp: westminster XWN 18288/ XWN 18379/XWN 18458/WL 5308 lp: nixa WLP 5308 lp: vega 10206 lp: whitehall WL 30016/WH 20060 lp: heliodor 478 016 lp: ducretet 270CW-071 lp: emi XLP 20068/1C045 91171

piano concerto no 2

vienna 28 june- 8 july 1954	vienna state opera orchestra badura-skoda	lp: westminster XWN 18288/WL 5308 lp: nixa WLP 5308 lp: whitehall WL 30016/WH 20060 lp: ricordi MRC 5008 lp: heliodor 478 016 lp: ducretet 270CW-071 lp: emi XLP 20068/1C045 91171

AARON COPLAND (1900-1990)

appalachian spring

new york 7 october 1945	nypso	cd: as-disc AS 546

a lincoln portrait

new york 20 february- 5 march 1946	nypso spencer	78: columbia (usa) X 266 lp: columbia (usa) ML 2042

FRANCOIS COUPERIN (1668-1733)

la sultane, arrangement from trio sonata in d minor

new york   nypso   cd: as-disc AS 535
29 october   cd: radio years RY 52
1944

CLAUDE DEBUSSY (1862-1918)

la mer

cleveland 10 january 1940	cleveland orchestra	columbia unpublished
cleveland 29 december 1941	cleveland orchestra	78: columbia (usa) M 531 lp: columbia (usa) ML 2005/ RL 6628/HL 7058 cd: dante LYS 276

fêtes/nocturnes

new york 29 april 1950	columbia so	45: columbia (usa) A 1003 lp: columbia (usa) ML 4337/CL 746

clair de lune/suite bergamasque

new york 16 february 1950	columbia so	45: columbia (usa) A 1002 45: philips SBF 130/S313 424F lp: columbia (usa) ML 4311/CL 726 lp: Philips SBL 5204/S04601L

GRIGORAS DINICU (1889-1949)

hora staccato, arrangement for orchestra

new york 28 april 1950	columbia so	45: columbia (usa) A 1003/A 1560 lp: columbia (usa) ML 4337/CL 746

ANTONIN DVORAK (1841-1904)

symphony no 9 "from the new world"

walthamstow 5-9 october 1954	rpo	lp: westminster XWN 18295/WL 5370/ WM 1031/WMS 1031 lp: westminster (germany) P285 lp: vega C30S-250 lp: ricordi MRC 5009 lp: heliodor 478 023 cd: mca MVCW 18014 second movement lp: westminster XWN 18735 orchestra described for this recording as philharmonic symphony orchestra

cello concerto

new york 7 january 1945	nypso rose	cd: as-disc AS 630 cd: legends LGD 141 cd: iron needle IN 1338

slavonic dances

walthamstow 8 april- 27 may 1955	rpo	lp: westminster XWN 2204/ XWN 18108-18109 lp: vega C30S-161-162 excerpts lp: nixa WLP 20013 lp: heliodor 478 053 lp: emi XLP 20063 cd: mca MVCW 18005

GEORGE ENESCU (1881-1955)

rumanian rhapsody no 1

new york 20 february- 5 march 1946	nypso	lp: columbia (usa) ML 2057/ RL 6628/HL 7058

GABRIEL FAURE (1845-1924)

ballade pour piano et orchestre

walthamstow 11 october 1954	rpo demus	westminster unpublished

MANUEL DE FALLA (1876-1946)

el sombrero de 3 picos, ballet suites 1 and 2

london   rpo   lp: hmv ALP 1688/ASD 281
28 april-   lp: hmv (france) CTRE 6130
5 may   lp: capitol G 7176/SG 7176
1958   lp: angel 60021
                                        lp: emi CFP 40261/1C045 01657
                                        cd: emi CZS 568 7422
                                        excerpts
                                        lp: capitol P 8564/SP 8564

ritual fire dance/el amor brujo

london   rpo   lp: hmv ALP 1688/ASD 281
16 september   lp: hmv (france) CTRE 6130
1957   lp: capitol G 7176/SG 7176
                                        lp: angel 60021
                                        lp: emi CFP 40261/1C045 01657
                                        cd: emi CZS 568 7422

CESAR FRANCK (1822-1890)

symphony in d minor

new york 2 january 1939	nbc so	78: world's greatest music SR 33/SR 38 78: music appreciation society 112
new york 30 december 1945	nypso	cd: as-disc AS 630 cd: iron needle IN 1338 cd: legends LGD 141
new york 29 april 1950	columbia so	45: columbia (usa) A 1003 lp: columbia (usa) ML 4337 second movement only
vienna 27 june- 11 july 1954	vienna state opera orchestra	lp: westminster XWN 18291 lp: nixa WLP 5311 lp: ducretet 320CW-094 lp: ricordi MRC 5010 lp: music appreciation MAS 5711 cd: mca MVCW 18003

variations symphoniques pour piano et orchestre

walthamstow 8 april 1955	rpo badura-skoda	lp: westminster XWN 18521/ WST 14251/WG 18001/LAB 7030 lp: nixa WLP 20026 lp: whitehall WH 20052 lp: vega C35S-116 lp: heliodor 480 009 lp: world records T 376/ST 376 <u>orchestra described for this recording as philharmonic symphony orchestra</u>

le chasseur maudit

vienna 27 june- 11 july 1954	vienna state opera orchestra	lp: westminster XWN 18291 lp: nixa WLP 5311 lp: ducretet 320CW-094 lp: ricordi MRC 5010 cd: mca MVCW 18003

GEORGE GERSHWIN (1898-1937)

an american in paris

new york 1940s	nypso	cd: as-disc AS 546
new york 11 december 1944	nypso	78: columbia (usa) X 246 78: columbia (italy) GQX 11161-11162 78: afrs basic music library C 329 45: philips NBE 11125 lp: columbia 33S 1003 lp: columbia (usa) ML 4026/ML 4879/ CL 700/CS 8641/XSM 55976 lp: columbia (austria) VS 801 lp: columbia (france) FA 1001 lp: columbia (italy) 33QS 1002

porgy and bess, excerpt (summertime)

new york 1 may 1950	columbia so rowe	45: columbia (usa) A 1003 lp: columbia (usa) ML 4337/CL 746

UMBERTO GIORDANO (1867-1948)

andrea chenier, excerpt (la mamma morta)

los angeles 18 july 1950	los angeles po roman	lp: ed smith EJS 426

REINHOLD GLIERE (1875-1956)

russian sailors' dance/the red poppy

new york	columbia so	45: columbia (usa) A 1003/A 1560
29 april		lp: columbia (usa) ML 4337/CL 746
1950		

MIKHAIL GLINKA (1804-1857)

ruslan and lyudmila, overture

london	rpo	lp: hmv ALP 1711/ASD 288
		lp: capitol G 7182/SG 7182
		lp: angel 60074
		cd: emi CZS 568 7422

CHRISTOPH WILLIBALD GLUCK (1714-1787)

orfeo ed euridice, excerpt (che faro)

new york	cleveland	lp: ed smith EJS 482
22 november	orchestra	
1936	swarthout	

MORTON GOULD (1913-1996)

spirituals

new york 9 may 1946	nypso	78: columbia (usa) M 832 lp: columbia (usa) ML 2042

CHARLES GOUNOD (1818-1893)

faust, excerpt (avant de quitter ces lieux)

warsaw 1930s	orchestra mossakowski <u>sung in polish</u>	lp: muza XL 0112

ENRIQUE GRANADOS (1867-1916)

andaluza/danzas espanolas

london 16 september 1957	rpo	lp: hmv ALP 1688/ASD 281 lp: hmv (france) CTRE 6130 lp: capitol G 7176/P 8564/ SG 7176/SP 8564 lp: angel 60021 lp: emi CFP 40261/1C045 01657 cd: emi CZS 568 7422

EDVARD GRIEG (1843-1907)

piano concerto

walthamstow	rpo	lp: westminster XWN 18231/
29-30	boukoff	XWN 18725
april		lp: ricordi MRC 5039
1955		<u>first movement</u>
		lp: heliodor 476 008
		<u>orchestra described for this recording</u>
		<u>as philharmonic symphony orchestra</u>

peer gynt, suites 1 and 2

walthamstow	rpo	lp: westminster XWN 18231/LAB 7014
8 april-		lp: westminster (germany) P 254
27 may		lp: vega C35S-028
1955		lp: ricordi MRC 5039
		lp: heliodor 476 007
		lp: emi MFP 2097
		cd: mca MVCW 18014
		<u>excerpts</u>
		lp: westminster XWN 18375/
		XWN 18890

JACQUES IBERT (1890-1962)

escales

new york	nypso	v-disc: 886-887
27 february		78: columbia (usa) X 263
1945		78: columbia (canada) J 90
		lp: columbia 33C 1027
		lp: columbia (france) 33FC 1003
		lp: columbia (usa) ML 2093/RL 6629

MIKHAIL IPPOLITOV-IVANOV (1859-1935)

caucasian sketches

walthamstow	rpo	lp: westminster XWN 18542/LAB 7039
27 april		lp: whitehall WH 20095
1955		lp: vega C35S-156
		lp: ricordi MRC 5020
		cd: mca MVCW 18009
		orchestra described for this recording
		as philharmonic symphony orchestra

ARMAS JAERNEFELT (1869-1958)

praeludium

cleveland	cleveland	78: columbia (usa) M 514
28 december	orchestra	cd: dante LYS 146
1941		

JEROME KERN (1885-1945)

showboat, scenario for orchestra

cleveland 29 december 1941	cleveland orchestra	78: columbia (usa) M 495

ARAM KHACHATURIAN (1803-1878)

gayaneh, ballet suite

chicago 18 november- 13 december 1947	chicago so	78: victor M 1212 45: victor WDM 1212/CAE 194 lp: victor CAL 215 <u>excerpts</u> 78: victor 12-0209 78: victor (italy) DV 16303 45: victor 49-0137 lp: victor DPL1-0212

ZOLTAN KODALY (1882-1867)

hary janos, suite

walthamstow	rpo	lp: westminster XWN 18775/LAB 7034
8 april-		lp: nixa WLP 20028
27 may		lp: whitehall WH 20052
1955		lp: vega C30A-099/C30A-444
		lp: heliodor 480 009
		lp: world records T 396
		cd: mca MVCW 18007
		orchestra described for this recording
		as philharmonic symphony orchestra

dances of galanta

walthamstow	rpo	lp: westminster XWN 18775
8 april-		lp: nixa WLP 20028
27 may		lp: whitehall WH 20052
1955		lp: vega C30A-099/C30A-444
		lp: heliodor 480 008/480 009
		lp: world records T 396
		cd: mca MCVW 18007
		orchestra described for this recording
		as philharmonic symphony orchestra

dances of marosszek

walthamstow	rpo	lp: westminster XWN 18775
8 april-		lp: nixa WLP 20028
27 may		lp: whitehall WH 20052
1955		lp: vega C30A-444
		lp: world records T 396
		cd: mca MCVW 18007
		orchestra described for this recording
		as philharmonic symphony orchestra

ERICH WOLFGANG KORNGOLD (1897-1957)

die tote stadt, excerpt (glück, das mir verblieb)

los angeles   los angeles po   lp: ed smith EJS 426
18 july   roman
1950

FRANZ   LISZT   (1811-1886)

hungarian rhapsody no 2

new york   columbia so   45: columbia (usa) A 1002
15 february   lp: columbia (usa) ML 4311/AL2/CL726
1950   lp: philips S04601L/GBL 5568/
                                             G03561L

GUSTAV MAHLER (1860-1911)

das lied von der erde

new york	nypso	lp: baton 1001
19 november	thorborg,	cd: as-disc AS 528
1944	kullmann	cd: grammofono AB 78623

BOHUSLAV MARTINU (1890-1959)

memorial to lidice

new york	nypso	78: us office for war information
1944		OWI 13-W 21-24

FELIX   MENDELSSOHN-BARTHOLDY   (1809-1847)

symphony   no 3   "scotch"

chicago	chicago so	78: victor M 1285
18 november-		45: victor WDM 1285
13 december		lp: victor LM 1053
1947		cd: chicago so centenary set
		cd: dante LYS 241
		<u>second movement</u>
		lp: victor DPM4-0210

a   midsummer   night's   dream,   suite (overture,   scherzo,   intermezzo, nocturne   and   wedding   march)

cleveland	cleveland	78: columbia LX 25021-25024
28 december	orchestra	78: columbia (usa) M 504
1941-		lp: columbia ML 4032/RL 3047/
22 february		P 14124
1942		cd: dante LYS 258
		<u>nocturne only</u>
		78: us office for war information
		OWI 14
		<u>incorrectly described by dante as a</u>
		<u>live performance</u>

a   midsummer   night's   dream,   scherzo

new york	columbia so	45: columbia (usa) A 1002/A 1530
16 february		45: philips NBE 11075/N 409538 E
1950		lp: columbia (usa) ML 4311/CL 726
		lp: philips SBL 5204/S04601L/
		GBL 5568/G03561L

WOLFGANG AMADEUS MOZART (1756-1791)

symphony no 35 "haffner"

new york 1944-1946	nypso	cd: as-disc AS 611

piano concerto no 13

new york 27 october 1946	nypso landowska	lp: discocorp IGI 331 lp: discophilia DIS 278 lp: desmar IPA 106-107 cd: as-disc AS 527 cd: iron needle IN 1336 cd: piano library PL 283

piano concerto no 22

new york 2 december 1945	nypso landowska	lp: discocorp IGI 331 lp: discophilia DIS 278 lp: desmar IPA 106-107 cd: as-disc AS 527 cd: iron needle IN 1336 cd: piano library PL 283

piano concerto no 23

new york 3 march 1946	nypso schnabel	lp: discocorp BWS 717 lp: MKR 1004 cd: as-disc AS 611 cd: music and arts CD 632

bassoon concerto

vienna	vienna state	lp: westminster XWN 18237
3 july	opera orchestra	lp: nixa WLP 5307
1954	oehlberger	lp: whitehall WH 20060
		lp: heliodor 478 083
		cd: mca MCVW 18009
		also issued on cd by toshiba

clarinet concerto

vienna	vienna state	lp: westminster XWN 18237
3 july	opera orchestra	lp: nixa WLP 5307
1954	wlach	lp: whitehall WH 20060
		lp: heliodor 478 083
		cd: mca MCVW 18009
		also issued on cd by toshiba

eine kleine nachtmusik

new york	nypso	cd: as-disc AS 611
1944-1946		

MODEST MUSSORGSKY (1839-1881)

pictures at an exhibtion, arranged by ravel

new york 12 march 1945	nypso	78: columbia (usa) M 641 78: afrs basic music library C 239-240 lp: columbia (usa) ML 4033/RL 3119/ HL 7075 cd: dante LYS 176
walthamstow 25-27 april 1955	rpo	lp: westminster XWN 18721/LAB 7019 lp: whitehall WH 20095 lp: vega C35S-130 lp: heliodor 480 007 lp: emi XLP 20063 cd: mca MCVW 18009 orchestra described for this recording as philharmonic symphony orchestra

night on bare mountain

walthamstow 6 may 1955	rpo	lp: westminster XWN 18542/LAB 7034 lp: whitehall WH 20095 lp: ricordi MRC 5020 cd: mca MCVW 18009 orchestra described for this recording as philharmonic symphony orchestra

boris godunov

rome 22 october 1955	rai roma orchestra and chorus corsi, picchi, christoff, modesti sung in italian	lp: hope records HOPE 220 excerpts lp: longanesi GML 10

khovantschina

rome 14 june 1958	rai roma orchestra and chorus companeez, picchi, petri, christoff <u>sung in italian</u>	cd: datum DAT 12320

khovantschina, prelude

cleveland 20 december 1939	cleveland orchestra	columbia unpublished
cleveland 26 december 1940	cleveland orchestra	78: columbia (usa) M 478 cd: dante LYS 176
london 27 april 1958	rpo	lp: hmv ALP 1711/ASD 288 lp: capitol G 7182/SG 7182 lp: angel 60074/6061 cd: emi CZS 568 7422

sorochintski fair, gopak

new york 20 february 1946	nypso	78: columbia (usa) M 641 cd: dante LYS 176

JACQUES OFFENBACH (1819-1880)

orfée aux enfers, overture

new york	columbia so	45: columbia (usa) A 1003
1 may		lp: columbia (usa) ML 4337/AL2/CL746
1950		

NICOLO PAGANINI (1782-1840)

violin concerto no 1

new york	nypso	columbia unpublished
12 february	francescatti	
1945		

SERGEI PROKOFIEV (1891-1953)

symphony no 1 "classical"

walthamstow 2 may 1955	rpo	lp: westminster XWN 18701/LAB 7017 lp: whitehall WH 20029 lp: heliodor 480 008 cd: mca MVCW 18012 orchestra described for this recording as philharmonic symphony orchestra

symphony no 5

new york 22 october 1946	nypso	78: columbia LX 1147-1151 78: columbia (usa) M 661 lp: columbia (usa) ML 4037 lp: philips A01105L
rome 11 may 1957	rai roma orchestra	cd: stradivarius STR 13613

alexander nevsky

rome 22 march 1958	rai roma orchestra and chorus companeez sung in italian	cd: stradivarius STR 10035

l'amour des 3 oranges, suite

walthamstow 6 may 1955	rpo	lp: westminster XWN 18701/LAB 7017 lp: whitehall WH 20029 lp: heliodor 480 008 cd: mca MVCW 18012 <u>march only</u> lp: westminster XWN 18599 <u>orchestra described for this recording</u> <u>as philharmonic symphony orchestra</u>

l'amour des 3 oranges, march and scherzo

new york 29 april 1950	columbia so	45: columbia (usa) A 1003/A 1560 lp: columbia (usa) ML 4337/CL 746

peter and the wolf

walthamstow
2 may
1955
	rpo
	moore
		lp: westminster XWN 18525/
		    XWN 18701/XWN 18737/
		    WST 14040/WGS 8107
		lp: whitehall WH 20040
		lp: music guild MS 158
		lp: record club of america SEY 1
		lp: world records T 381/ST 381
		cd: mca MVCW 18012
		<u>orchestra described for this recording</u>
		<u>as philharmonic symphony orchestra</u>

GIACOMO PUCCINI (1858-1924)

manon lescaut, excerpt (in quelle trine morbide)

los angeles 18 july 1950	los angeles po roman	lp: ed smith EJS 426

SERGEI RACHMANINOV (1873-1943)

symphony no 2

new york 15 january 1945	nypso	78: columbia (usa) M 569 lp: columbia (usa) RL 3049/HL 7101

piano concerto no 2

new york 2 january 1946	nypso sandor	78: columbia (usa) M 605 78: columbia (canada) 15902-15905 lp: columbia (usa) RL 3052/HL 7059

piano concerto no 2, first movement

new york 17 february 1950	columbia so pennario	45: columbia (usa) A 1002 lp: columbia (usa) ML 4311/CL 726 lp: philips S04601L/GBL 5568/ G03561L

rhapsody on a theme of paganini

new york 28 october 1945	nypso kapell	cd: pearl GEMMCD 9194

MAURICE   RAVEL   (1875-1937)

daphnis et chloé, second suite

cleveland 29 december 1941	cleveland orchestra	78: columbia (usa) X 230 lp: columbia (usa) ML 4039/ 　　ML 4884/P 14127

alborada del gracioso

cleveland 29 december 1941	cleveland orchestra	columbia unpublished
cleveland 22 february 1942	cleveland orchestra	78: columbia (usa) 11910D 78: columbia (canada) 15686

rapsodie espagnole

cleveland 26 december 1940- 14 april 1941	cleveland orchestra	78: columbia (usa) X 234 78: columbia (canada) 　　15687-15688 lp: columbia (usa) ML 4039/ 　　ML 4884/P 14127 cd: dante LYS 276

NIKOLAI RIMSKY-KORSAKOV (1844-1908)

scheherazade

cleveland 20 december 1939	cleveland orchestra	78: columbia (usa) M 398 78: columbia (argentina) 266008-266012 78: columbia (japan) JN 602-606 lp: columbia (usa) RL 3001/HL 7051 cd: cleveland orchestra TCO93-75 cd: dante LYS 161 first ever recording made in severance hall

scheherazade, third movement

new york 1 may 1950	columbia so	45: columbia (usa) A 1003 lp: columbia (usa) ML 4337/CL 746

piano concerto

walthamstow 8 april 1955	rpo badura-skoda	lp: westminster XWN 18521/ W 18001/WST 14251 lp: whitehall WH 20052 lp: vega C35S-116 lp: heliodor 480 009 lp: world records T 376/ST 376 orchestra described for this recording as philharmonic symphony orchestra

russian easter festival overture

london 28 april- 6 may 1958	rpo	lp: hmv ALP 1711/ASD 288 lp: capitol G 7182/SG 7182 lp: angel 60074 cd: emi CZS 568 7422

GIOACHINO ROSSINI (1792-1868)

guillaume tell, overture

new york 14 february 1950	columbia so	45: columbia (usa) A 1002/A 1591 lp: columbia (usa) ML 4311/CL 726 lp: philips SBL 5204/S04601L/ GBL 5568/G03561L

ANTON RUBINSTEIN (1829-1894)

piano concerto no 4

new york 5 march 1944	nypso hofmann	lp: international piano library GNR 107 lp: international piano archives IPA 500 first movement lp: international piano library GNR 111

CAMILLE SAINT-SAENS (1835-1921)

piano concerto no 4

new york 5 february 1945	nypso casadesus	78: columbia (usa) M 566 lp: columbia (usa) ML 4246/P 14156 lp: coronet (australia) KLC 582 cd: radio years RY 52

ARNOLD SCHOENBERG (1874-1951)

ode to napoleon

new york 26 november 1944	nypso harrell	cd: nypso historic broadcasts

FRANZ SCHUBERT (1797-1828)

symphony no 8 "unfinished"

walthamstow
25-28
september
1956
	rpo	lp: westminster XWN 18700/LAB 7044/
		    WMS 1031/WST 14052/
		    WST 16006/WGS 8123
		lp: westminster (germany) P 254
		lp: music guild MS 173
		lp: ricordi MRC 5028
		lp: heliodor 476 002
		lp: emi 1C045 90320
		cd: mca MCD 80096/MVCW 18010
		excerpts
		lp: westminster XWN 18738/
		    XWN 18822
		orchestra described for this recording
		as philharmonic symphony orchestra

ROBERT SCHUMANN (1810-1856)

piano concerto

vienna	vienna state	lp: westminster XWN 18290/
27 june-	opera orchestra	XWN 18458
11 july	demus	lp: whitehall WH 20072
1954		lp: nixa WLP 5310
		lp: ducretet 270CW-079
		lp: ricordi MRC 5005
		lp: heliodor 478 013

introduction and allegro appassionato for piano and orchestra

vienna	vienna state	lp: westminster XWN 18290
27 june-	opera orchestra	lp: whitehall WH 20072
11 july	demus	lp: nixa WLP 5310
1954		lp: ricordi MRC 5005
		lp: heliodor 478 013

konzertstück for piano and orchestra

vienna	vienna state	lp: westminster XWN 18290
27 june-	opera orchestra	lp: whitehall WH 20072
11 july	demus	lp: nixa WLP 5310
1954		lp: ricordi MRC 5005
		lp: heliodor 478 013

ALEXANDER SCRIABIN (1872-1915)

symphony no 3 "divine poem"

new york 31 december 1938	nbc so	cd: dante LYS 176
rome 22 february 1958	rai roma orchestra	cd: stradivarius STR 13613 cd: datum DAT 12306

DIMITRI   SHOSTAKOVICH   (1906-1975)

symphony no 1

cleveland 14 april 1941	cleveland orchestra	78: columbia (usa) M 472
		 78: columbia (australia)
		     LOX 558-561
		 lp: columbia (usa) ML 4101/ML 4881/
		     P 14142/P 14191
		 lp: philips A01179L
		 cd: dante LYS 139

symphony no 5

cleveland 22 february 1942	cleveland orchestra	78: columbia (usa) M 520 78: columbia (canada) D 119 lp: columbia (usa) ML 4042/ RL 6625/P 14128 cd: dante LYS 139
walthamstow 2-14 october 1954	rpo	lp: westminster XWN 18001/ W 9731/OC 8014 lp: whitehall WH 20092 lp: nixa WLP 20004 lp: vega C30A-074 lp: ricordi MRC 5040 cd: mca MCD 80112/MVCW 18008 second movement also appeared on westminster hi-fi test record; orchestra described for this recording as philharmonic symphony orchestra

symphony no 8

new york 15 october 1944	nypso	cd: as-disc AS 538/AS 630

symphony no 10

rome 18 march 1955	rai roma orchestra	cd: stradivarius STR 10035

JEAN   SIBELIUS   (1865-1957)

symphony   no   2

turin date not confirmed	rai torino orchestra	cd: datum DAT 12306

symphony   no   4

new york 5 march 1946	nypso	78: columbia (usa) M 665

symphony   no   5

cleveland 28 december 1941	cleveland orchestra	78: columbia (usa) M 514 78: columbia (canada) D 118 lp: columbia (usa) ML 4043/ML 4881/ P 14129/P 14191 lp: philips A01179L cd: dante LYS 146

finlandia

cleveland 20 december 1939	cleveland orchestra	78: columbia (usa) 11178D 78: columbia (canada) 20016

JOHANN STRAUSS II (1825-1899)

an der schönen blauen donau, waltz

walthamstow	rpo	lp: westminster XWN 18500/LAB 7026
9 may		lp: whitehall WH 20062
1955		lp: vega C30A-083
		lp: ricordi MRC 5040
		orchestra described for this recording
		as philharmonic symphony orchestra

frühlingsstimmen, waltz

walthamstow	rpo	45: ricordi ERC 25002
11 may		45: heliodor 466 002
1955		lp: westminster XWN 18500/LAB 7026
		lp: whitehall WH 20062
		lp: vega C30A-083
		orchestra described for this recording
		as philharmonic symphony orchestra

g'schichten aus dem wienerwald, waltz

| walthamstow
11 may
1955 | rpo | 45: ricordi ERC 25002
lp: westminster XWN 18500/
     LAB 7025/LAB 7026
lp: whitehall WH 20062
<u>orchestra described for this recording</u>
<u>as philharmonic symphony orchestra</u> |

kaiserwalzer

| walthamstow
10 may
1955 | rpo | 45: heliodor 466 002
lp: westminster XWN 18500/LAB 7026
lp: whitehall WH 20062
lp: vega C30A-083
lp: ricordi MRC 5040

<u>orchestra described for this recording</u>
<u>as philharmonic symphony orchestra</u> |

rosen aus dem süden, waltz

| walthamstow
9 may
1955 | rpo | lp: westminster XWN 18500/LAB 7026
lp: whitehall WH 20062
lp: vega C30A-083
lp: ricordi MRC 5040
<u>orchestra described for this recording</u>
<u>as philharmonic symphony orchestra</u> |

RICHARD STRAUSS (1864-1949)

also sprach zarathustra

chicago 17 november- 13 december 1947	chicago so	78: victor M 1258 45: victor WDM 1258 lp: victor LM 1060/DPL1-0245 lp: hmv (france) FALP 179 lp: chicago symphony orchestra

dance suite after couperin

london 7 may 1958	philharmonia	lp: hmv ALP 1605/ASD 270 lp: hmv (italy) QALP 10292/ASDQ 5285 lp: capitol G 7147/SG 7147 lp: angel 60030 lp: world records T 723/ST 723 lp: emi 1C053 01212 cd: emi CZS 568 7422

don juan

walthamstow 19 april 1955	rpo	lp: westminster XWN 18680/ 　　　WGM 8314/LAB 7016 lp: nixa WLP 20027 lp: whitehall WH 20067 lp: vega C35S-160 lp: heliodor 476 003 cd: mca MVCW 18012 orchestra described for this recording as philharmonic symphony orchestra

elektra

new york	nypso	lp: ed smith EJS 145/UORC 322
21 march	pauly,	lp: international record collector
1937	szantho,	cd: eklipse EKRCD 17
	boerner,	preserved recording contains only
	jagel, huehn	elektra's scenes

ein heldenleben

cleveland	cleveland	78: columbia (usa) M 441
12 january-	orchestra	lp: columbia (usa) RL 3048
26 december		cd: dante LYS 274
1940		

der rosenkavalier, orchestral suite (1945)

walthamstow	rpo	lp: westminster XWN 18680/
18-19		XWN 18736/LAB 7025/WGM 8314
april		lp: whitehall WH 20067
1955		cd: mca MVCW 18006
		excerpts
		lp: heliodor 476 010
		orchestra described for this recording
		as philharmonic symphony orchestra

der rosenkavalier, act 3 waltz sequence

cleveland	cleveland	78: columbia (usa) 11542D
26 december	orchestra	lp: columbia (usa) ML 4045/
1940		ML 4884/P 14131
		lp: telarc "cleveland orchestra on stage"

salome, dance of the 7 veils

cleveland 22 february 1942	cleveland orchestra	78: columbia (usa) 11781D lp: columbia (usa) ML 4884/P 14131
london 15 september 1957- 29 april 1958	philharmonia	lp: hmv ALP 1605/ASD 270 lp: hmv (italy) QALP 10292/ASDQ 5285 lp: capitol G 7147/SG 7147 lp: angel 60030 lp: world records T 723/ST 723 cd: emi CZS 568 7422

till eulenspiegels lustige streiche

cleveland 26 december 1940	cleveland orchestra	78: columbia (usa) X 210 lp: columbia (usa) ML 4045/ML 4884 cd: dante LYS 274 /P 14131
walthamstow 19 april 1955	rpo	lp: westminster XWN 18650/ WGM 8314/LAB 7016 lp: nixa WLP 20027 lp: whitehall WH 20067 lp: heliodor 476 003 cd: mca MVCW 18012 orchestra described for this recording as philharmonic symphony orchestra

tod und verklärung

london 14 september 1957- 29 april 1958	philharmonia	lp: hmv ALP 1605/ASD 270 lp: hmv (italy) QALP 10292/ASDQ 5285 lp: capitol G 7147/SG 7147 lp: angel 60030 lp: world records T 723/ST 723 lp: emi 1C053 01212 cd: emi CZS 568 7422

IGOR STRAVINSKY (1882-1972)

le sacre du printemps

florence march 1953	maggio musicale orchestra	lp: cetra DOC 74

l'oiseau de feu, suite

rome date not confirmed	rai roma orchestra	cd: datum DAT 12306

KAROL SZYMANOWSKI (1882-1937)

violin concerto no 2

rome 18 march 1955	rai roma orchestra szeryng	cd: datum DAT 12306

stabat mater

turin 18 april 1958	rai torino orchestra and chorus	cd: datum DAT 12306 cd: dante LYS 155

PIOTR TCHAIKOVSKY (1840-1893)

symphony no 4

new york 2 january 1939	nbc so	78: world's greatest music SR 23/SR 27 78: music appreciation society 109
new york 13 january 1946	nypso	cd: as-disc AS 520

walthamstow
20-25
september
1956
	rpo	lp: westminster XWN 18541/
		    WMS 1020/WST 14006
		lp: whitehall WH 20030
		lp: heliodor 428 004/478 019
		lp: world records T 363/ST 363
		cd: mca MVCW 14010-14011/
		    MCD 80101
		third movement
		lp: westminster XWN 18738
		orchestra described for this recording
		as philharmonic symphony orchestra

symphony no 5

cleveland 20 december 1939- 8 january 1940	cleveland orchestra	78: columbia (usa) M 406 78: afrs basic music library C 223-224/SSL 2523-2524 lp: columbia (usa) ML 4052/P 14135 cd: dante LYS 208
new york 28 october 1945	nypso	cd: as-disc AS 514

walthamstow
2-3
october
1954
	rpo	lp: westminster XWN 18355/
		    WM 1020/WMS 1020/WG 18008/
		    LAB 8001-8003
		lp: vega C30A-036
		lp: heliodor 478 020
		lp: emi 1C045 90341
		cd: mca MVCW 14010-14011
		second movement
		lp: westminster XWN 18736
		orchestra described for this recording
		as philharmonic symphony orchestra

symphony no 6 "pathétique"

new york	nypso	78: columbia DX 1205-1209
11 december		78: columbia (usa) M 558
1944		78: afrs basic music library C122-124
		lp: columbia (usa) ML 4051/RL 3118/
		HL 7052/P 14134

walthamstow	rpo	lp: westminster XWN 18048/
3-4		WM 1020/WMS 1020
october		lp: westminster (germany) P 320
1954		lp: heliodor 478 021
		lp: emi 1C045 90342
		cd: mca MVCW 14010-14011
		third movement
		lp: westminster XWN 18736
		orchestra described for this recording
		as philharmonic symphony orchestra

piano concerto no 1

new york	nypso	cd: as-disc AS 519
24 march	rubinstein	cd: legends LGD 127
1946		

violin concerto

walthamstow	rpo	lp: westminster XWN 18397/
22-25	morini	WST 14017/WM 1011/WST 1011
september		lp: westminster (germany) P 321
1956		lp: vega C30S-152
		lp: ricordi MRC 5030
		lp: heliodor 420 002/476 004
		lp: emi XLP 20053/SXLP 20053
		cd: mca MCD 80101
		orchestra described for this recording
		as philharmonic symphony orchestra

suite no 4 "mozartiana"

new york 2 december 1945	nypso	cd: as-disc	+

new york 27 february 1945	nypso	78: columbia (usa) X 248 lp: columbia (usa) ML 4048/P 14132

1812 overture

cleveland 14 april 1941	cleveland orchestra	78: columbia LX 932-933 78: columbia (usa) X 205 lp: columbia (usa) ML 4049/RL 6626/ HL 7056/P 14133 cd: dante LYS 208 it is generally thought that although this recording bears rodzinski's name, it was actually conducted by his assistant rudolf wingwall; dante incorrectly states conductor to be walter hendl

serenade for strings, waltz

new york 17 february 1950	columbia so	45: columbia (usa) A 1002 45: philips NBE 11075/N409 538E lp: columbia (usa) ML 4311/CL 726 lp: philips SBL 5204/S04601L/ GBL 5568/G03561L

marche slave

cleveland 26 december 1940	cleveland orchestra	78: columbia (usa) 11567D 78: columbia (argentina) 266152 cd: dante LYS 208 it is generally thought that although this recording bears rodzinski's name, it was actually conducted by his assistant rudolf wingwall

romeo and juliet, fantasy overture

cleveland 26 december 1940	cleveland orchestra	78: columbia (usa) M 478 lp: columbia (usa) ML 4049/RL 6626/ HL 7056/P 14133 cd: dante LYS 161
london 27 april- 27 may 1958	rpo	lp: hmv ALP 1711/ASD 288 lp: capitol G 7182/SG 7182 lp: angel 60074 cd: emi CZS 568 7422 excerpts lp: capitol P 8563/PCR 8588/ SP 8563/SPCR 8588

evgeny onegin, polonaise

| new york
28 october
1945 | nypso | cd: as-disc AS 514 |

evgeny onegin, excerpt (faint echo of my youth)

| warsaw
1930s | orchestra
dobosz
<u>sung in polish</u> | lp: muza XL 0111 |

none but the lonely heart

| new york
15 february
1950 | columbia so
lipton | 45: columbia (usa) A 1002
45: philips NBE 11075
lp: columbia (usa) ML 4311
lp: philips SBL 5204 |

swan lake, ballet suite

| vienna
27 june-
11 july
1954 | vienna state
opera orchestra | lp: westminster XWN 18223/
   XWN 18452
<u>excerpts</u>
lp: westminster XWN 18889
<u>recording not approved by rodzinski</u>
<u>but issued under a pseudonym</u> |

casse noisette

walthamstow
9-18
september
1956
	rpo	lp: westminster OPW 1205/WST 203/
		    WGS 8147
		lp: music guild MS 6202
		lp: sine qua non SQA 155
		lp: emi XLP 20059-20060/
		    SXLP 20059-20060
		cd: pickwick DUET 20
		cd: mca MCAD 29801
		excerpts
		45: ricordi ERC 25031
		lp: westminster XWN 18736/
		    XWN 18889/XWN 18897/
		    WST 14088/LAB 7042
		lp: music guild 178
		lp: heliodor 428 006/478 017
		lp: emi 1C045 91164
		orchestra described for this recording
		as philharmonic symphony orchestra

casse noisette, ballet suite

new york 1945-1946	nypso	cd: as-disc AS 520
new york 20 february- 5 march 1946	nypso	78: columbia DX 1342-1344 78: columbia (usa) M 627 lp: columbia (usa) ML 4048/P 14132 valse des fleurs 45: columbia (usa) A 1508
vienna 27 june- 11 july 1954	vienna state opera orchestra	lp: westminster XWN 18223 recording not approved by rodzinski but issued under a pseudonym

GIUSEPPE   VERDI   (1813-1901)

otello, excerpt (niun mi tema)

warsaw	orchestra	lp: muza XL 0110
1930s	gruszcynski	
	<u>sung in polish</u>	

RICHARD WAGNER (1813-1883)

siegfried idyll

new york 27 february 1945	nypso	78: columbia (usa) X 265 lp: columbia (usa) ML 4086

götterdämmerung, siegfried's rhine journey

walthamstow 14 april 1955	rpo	lp: westminster XWN 18453/LAB 7013 lp: nixa WLP 20024 lp: whitehall WH 20046 lp: heliodor 478 041 orchestra described for this recording as philharmonic symphony orchestra

götterdämmerung, siegfried's funeral march

new york 25 november 1945	nypso	cd: as-disc AS 545 cd: radio years RY 55
walthamstow 14 april 1955	rpo	lp: westminster XWN 18453/ XWN 18599/XWN 18822/LAB 7013 lp: nixa WLP 20024 lp: whitehall WH 20046 lp: ricordi MRC 5006 lp: heliodor 478 041 orchestra described for this recording as philharmonic symphony orchestra

lohengrin, prelude

vienna 6-11 march 1952	niederöster- reichisches tonkünstler- orchester	remington unpublished
walthamstow 17 april 1955	rpo	lp: westminster XWN 18602/LAB 7028 lp: nixa WLP 20025 lp: ricordi MRC 5026 lp: heliodor 466 018 orchestra described for this recording as philharmonic symphony orchestra

lohengrin, act 3 prelude

vienna 6-11 march 1952	niederöster- reichisches tonkünstler- orchester	remington unpublished

lohengrin, excerpt (einsam in trüben tagen)

new york 23 may 1945	nypso traubel	78: columbia LX 1026 78: columbia (usa) 12321D 45: columbia (usa) A 1550 lp: columbia (usa) Y 31735 lp: emi EX 769 7411 cd: emi CHS 769 7412 cd: metropolitan opera 214 cd: preiser 89120

lohengrin, excerpt (das süsse lied verhallt)

new york	nypso	78: columbia LX 991-992
18 may	traubel, baum	78: columbia (usa) X 261
1945		78: columbia (canada) 15968-15969
		lp: columbia (usa) ML 4055
		cd: preiser 89120

die meistersinger von nürnberg, overture

walthamstow	rpo	lp: westminster XWN 18602/LAB 7028
16 april		lp: nixa WLP 20024
1955		lp: ricordi MRC 5026
		lp: heliodor 466 018
		orchestra described for this recording
		as philharmonic symphony orchestra
walthamstow	rpo	lp: westminster XWN 18822
30 september		cd: mca MVCW 18014
1956		rehearsal performance at end of which
		rodzinski thanks the orchestra;
		orchestra described for this recording
		as philharmonic symphony orchestra

die meistersinger von nürnberg, act 3 suite (prelude, dance of apprentices and entry of masters)

walthamstow	rpo	lp: westminster XWN 18602/LAB 7028
16 april		lp: nixa WLP 20024
1955		lp: ricordi MRC 2056
		orchestra described for this recording
		as philharmonic symphony orchestra

parsifal, excerpt (von dorther kam das stöhnen)

new york	nypso	unpublished radio broadcast
1937	althouse,	
	list	

das rheingold, entry of the gods into valhalla

new york 25 november 1945	nypso	cd: as-disc AS 545 cd: radio years RY 55

siegfried, forest murmurs

new york 25 november 1945	nypso	cd: as-disc AS 545 cd: radio years RY 55

tannhäuser

rome 14-16 november 1957	rai roma orchestra and chorus brouwenstijn, wilfert, liebl, dickie, wächter, ernster	lp: melodram MEL 22 cd: datum DAT 12318 excerpts cd: myto MCD 93277

tannhäuser, overture

walthamstow 17 april 1955	rpo	lp: westminster XWN 18602/LAB 7035 lp: nixa WLP 20025 lp: ricordi MRC 5026 lp: heliodor 466 018 45! orchestra described for this recording as philharmonic symphony orchestra

tristan und isolde

florence may 1957	maggio musicale orchestra and chorus nilsson, hoffman, windgassen, neidlinger, rohr	lp: cetra DOC 20

tristan und isolde, prelude and liebestod

chicago 13 december 1947	chicago so	78: victor M 1230 45: victor WDM 1230 lp: victor LM 1060 <u>liebestod only</u> cd: rca/bmg GD 60206
walthamstow 14 april 1955	rpo	lp: westminster XWN 18453/ XWN 18822/LAB 7035 lp: nixa WLP 20025 lp: whitehall WH 20046 lp: ricordi MRC 5006 lp: heliodor 478 041 cd: mca MVCW 18013 <u>orchestra described for this recording as philharmonic symphony orchestra</u>

tristan und isolde, prelude

new york 22-23 may 1945	nypso	78: columbia LX 941-942 78: columbia (usa) M 573 lp: columbia (usa) RL 3047

tristan und isolde, act 3 prelude

new york 22-23 may 1945	nypso	78: columbia LX 941-942 78: columbia (usa) M 573 lp: columbia (usa) RL 3047
chicago 17 november 1947	chicago so	78: victor M 1258 45: victor WDM 1258

tristan und isolde, excerpt (doch nun von tristan?)

new york 23 may 1945	nypso traubel	78: columbia LX 942-943 78: columbia (usa) M 573 lp: columbia (usa) RL 3047/ 3216 0145

tristan und isolde, excerpt (mild und leise)

new york 23 may 1945	nypso traubel	78: columbia LX 945 78: columbia (usa) M 573 v-disc: 887 45: columbia (usa) A 1550 45: philips SBF 203 lp: columbia (usa) RL 3057/ 3216 0145/76005 cd: sony MK 46454 cd: preiser 89120

die walküre, act 3

new york	nypso	78: columbia LX 955-962
15-22	traubel,	78: columbia (usa) M 581
may	jessner,	78: columbia (canada) 15906-15913
1945	janssen	lp: columbia (usa) SL 5/SL 105/
		3226 0018/61452
		excerpt
		lp: metropolitan opera 214
new york	nypso	cd: as-disc AS 545
25 november	traubel,	cd: radio years RY 55
1945	doree,	
	janssen	

die walküre, excerpt (schläfst du, gast?)

new york	nypso	78: columbia (usa) M 618
25 may	traubel,	lp: columbia (usa) ML 4242/
1945	d'arcy	SL 5/SL 105/3226 0018

die walküre, ride of the valkyries

walthamstow	rpo	45: ricordi ERC 25007
14 april		45: vega C37S-089
1955		lp: westminster XWN 18453/LAB 7013
		lp: nixa WLP 20025
		lp: whitehall WH 20046
		lp: ricordi MRC 5006
		lp: heliodor 478 041
		orchestra described for this recording
		as philharmonic symphony orchestra

die walküre, magic fire music

walthamstow	rpo	45: ricordi ERC 25007
16 april		45: vega C37S-089
1955		lp: westminster XWN 18453/LAB 7013
		lp: nixa WLP 20024
		lp: whitehall WH 20046
		lp: ricordi MRC 2056
		lp: heliodor 466 013
		orchestra described for this recording
		as philharmonic symphony orchestra

CARL MARIA VON WEBER (1786-1826)

der freischütz, overture

| cleveland
22 february
1942 | cleveland
orchestra | 78: columbia (usa) 11817D |

JAROMIR WEINBERGER (1896-1967)

under the spreading chestnut tree, variations and fugue on an old english tune

| cleveland
10 january
1940 | cleveland
orchestra | 78: columbia (usa) X 161
78: columbia (canada) 20018-20019
lp: columbia (usa) P 12752 |

ERMANNO WOLF-FERRARI (1876-1948)

il segreto di susanna, overture

| new york
27 february
1945 | nypso | 78: columbia (usa) X 281/12905D
lp: columbia (usa) HL 7121/BM 13 |

MISCELLANEOUS

american national anthem

| new york
1944-1945 | nypso | cd: radio years RY 52 |

in camden nj on 6 october 1927 rodzinski recorded the piano illustrations for leopold stokowski's outline of themes which accompanied that conductor's victor recordings of franck symphony (78: victor M 22) and dvorak new world symphony (78: victor 6743; cd: biddulph WHL 27)

sergiu celibidache

1912-1996

discography compiled by john hunt

1946 / 6 - ZWEITER JAHRGANG - 20 Pf.

Neue Berliner Illustrierte

Aufnahme: W. Saeger

Sergiu Celibidache, der Dirigent der Berliner Philharmoniker

Der junge Rumäne studierte in Berlin an der Hochschule für Musik und an der Universität

(Zu unserem Bildbericht „Die Musiker Berlins")

JOHANN   SEBASTIAN   BACH   (1685-1750)

mass   in   b   minor

munich	munich po	cd: exclusive EX92T 33-34
18 november	mainz university	also issued by partita in japan
1990	bach choir	
	bonney, wulkopf,	
	schreier,	
	windmüller,	
	scharinger	

SVEN   ERIK   BAECK   (1919-1994)

intrada   for   orchestra

venice	la fenice	cd: originals SH 857
31 october	orchestra	
1965		

BELA BARTOK (1881-1945)

concerto for orchestra

london 1968	lso	cd: arlecchino ARLA 97
stuttgart 12 march 1976	sdr orchestra	cd: concert artists' recordings FED 053 also issued by audior in japan
stuttgart 10 february 1977	sdr orchestra	unpublished radio broadcast
munich 20 march 1995	munich po	cd: emi CDS 556 5172 also includes rehearsal extracts

rumanian folk dances

turin 9 january 1962	rai torino orchestra	cd: arkadia CD 526/CDHP 526
stuttgart date not confirmed	sdr orchestra	lp: rococo 2132 cd: arlecchino ARLA 97

LUDWIG VAN BEETHOVEN (1770-1827)

symphony no 1

munich 25 june 1989	munich po	cd: emi CDS 556 8372

symphony no 2

stockholm date not confirmed	swedish ro	cd: concert artists' recordings FED 071 cd: andromeda NAS 2503
munich 4 june 1996	munich po	cd: emi CDS 556 8372/CDC 556 8382 celibidache's final concert appearance

symphony no 3 "eroica"

stuttgart 21 march 1975	sdr orchestra	cd: concert artists' recordings FED 001 cd: arlecchino ARLA 103-106 cd: andromeda ANR 2501 FED 001 incorrectly dated 1971; also issued by meteor in japan, supposedly with rehearsal extracts
munich 1987	munich po	cd: meteor (japan) MCD 041 also issued by other labels in japan
munich 12 april 1987	munich po	cd: meteor (japan) MCD 041 cd: emi CDS 556 8372/CDC 556 8392
munich 16 january 1996	munich po	cd: audior (japan) AUDSE 501

symphony no 4

stockholm date not confirmed	swedish ro	cd: concert artists' recordings FED 071 cd: andromeda NAS 2503
munich 12 april 1987	munich po	cd: meteor (japan) MCD 052 cd: emi CDS 556 8372/CDC 556 8382 also issued by other labels in japan
munich 19 march 1995	munich po	cd: emi CDC 556 5212/CDS 556 5172

symphony no 5

stuttgart november 1972	sdr orchestra	unpublished radio broadcast of a rehearsal
nürnberg 24 november 1972	sdr orchestra	unpublished radio broadcast
stuttgart 10 february 1982	sdr orchestra	cd: exclusive EX92T 29-30 cd: arlecchino ARLA 103-106 cd: originals SH 811 also issued by meteor in japan
bonn 24-25 may 1989	munich po	cd: audior (japan) AUDSE 508
munich 28-31 may 1992	munich po	cd: emi CDC 556 5212/CDS 556 5172/ CDS 556 8872
tokyo 16 october 1992	munich po	cd: gewandhaus music circle (japan) CG 22

symphony no 6 "pastoral"

stuttgart 28 november 1975	sdr orchestra	unpublished radio broadcast
stuttgart 10 february 1982	sdr orchestra	lp: rococo 2153 cd: concert artists' recordings FED 050 cd: arlecchino ARLA 103-106 cd: exclusive EX92T 29-30 also issued by meteor in japan
munich 26 january 1993	munich po	cd: emi CDS 556 8372/CDC 556 8402
tokyo 26-30 april 1993	munich po	cd: gewandhaus music circle (japan) CG 18/CG 25 these issues may be two separate performances

symphony no 7

berlin 7 october 1957	berlin ro	cd: arkadia CD 734/CDGI 734 rehearsal of first and second movements
stuttgart 1964	sdr orchestra	lp: rococo 2148 cd: arkadia CD 737/CDGI 737
stuttgart 12 november 1981	sdr orchestra	cd: exclusive EX92T 29-30 cd: arlecchino ARLA 103-106 also issued by audior in japan
munich 20 january 1989	munich po	cd: audior (japan) AUDSE 2501-2502 cd: emi CDS.556 8372/CDC 556 8412 also issued by other labels in japan
munich june 1991	munich po	cd: galileo (japan) GL 5 also issued by other labels in japan

symphony no 8

stuttgart 21 march 1975	sdr orchestra	cd: audior (japan) AUDSE 518
munich 4 april 1995	munich po	cd: emi CDS 556 8372/CDC 556 8412

symphony no 9 "choral"

turin 28 march 1958	rai torino orchestra and chorus rizzoli, höffgen, munteanu, neagu	lp: rai torino limited edition cd: arkadia CD 613/CDHP 613
munich 17-19 march 1989	munich po and chorus donath, soffel, jerusalem, lika	cd: exclusive EX92T 15 cd: arlecchino ARLA 103-106 cd: emi CDS 556 8372/CDC 556 8422 also issued by partita in japan rehearsal extracts vhs video: teldec 4509 964383

piano concerto no 4

munich 17 march 1985	munich po perahia	cd: originals SH 811 also issued by other labels in japan; SH 811 incorrectly describes orchestra as sdr orchestra

piano concerto no 5 "emperor"

helsinki 20 may 1969	swedish ro michelangeli	lp: rococo 2047 cd: arkadia CD 592/CDHP 592/LE 951 cd: as-disc AS 320 cd: legends LGD 115 cd: notes PGP 11002
paris 16 october 1974	orchestre national michelangeli	lp: rococo 2126 lp: electrecord ECE 02600 cd: arkadia CD 609/CDHP 609 cd: music and arts CD 296 also issued by live classic best in japan
munich june 1991	munich po barenboim	cd: galileo (japan) GL 5

violin concerto

rome 30 january 1954	rai roma orchestra schneiderhan	lp: melodram MEL 201

coriolan overture

stuttgart 11 november 1982	sdr orchestra	cd: meteor (japan) MCD 044 also issued by gewandhaus music circle in japan

egmont overture

berlin 1950	bpo	lp: period SPL 716 vhs video: teldec 4509 957103/ 4509 964383 also issued on other vhs video and laserdisc labels in japan; original soundtrack recording for the film botschafter der musik, filmed to simulate performance taking place in ruins of alte philharmonie
turin 1968	rai torino orchestra	cd: concert artists' recordings FED 001 cd: andromeda ANR 2501
mannheim 13 october 1976	sdr orchestra	unpublished radio broadcast of a rehearsal
stuttgart 21 october 1976	sdr orchestra	unpublished radio broadcast

leonore no 3 overture

berlin 10 november 1946	bpo	cd: myto MCD 981 009 cd: tahra TAH 271 cd: grammofono AB 78774-78775
stuttgart date not confirmed	sdr orchestra	lp: rococo 2148 cd: originals SH 841
milan 28 april 1974	rai milano orchestra	cd: exclusive EX92T 29-30
munich 20 january 1989	munich po	cd: emi CDS 556 8372/CDC 556 8402 also issued by meteor in japan

ALBAN BERG (1885-1935)

violin concerto

mannheim 21 october 1976	sdr orchestra	unpublished radio broadcast sdr archive does not identify soloist in this performance

THEODOR BERGER (born 1905)

malincolia

stuttgart 21 november 1981	sdr orchestra	unpublished radio broadcast

HECTOR BERLIOZ (1803-1869)

symphonie fantastique

milan 22 february 1960	rai milano orchestra	lp: cetra LAR 22 cd: nuova era NE 2291/NE 2393-2391 second movement only
turin 29 april 1968	rai torino orchestra	cd: frequenz 041.021 cd: arkadia CD 437/CDMP 437 frequenz dated 20 july 1968
turin 24 october 1969	rai torino orchestra	cd: live classic best (japan) LCB 033/LCB 117
copenhagen 1970	danish ro	cd: documents LV 965

marche hongroise/la damnation de faust

stuttgart 9 june 1982	sdr orchestra	unpublished radio broadcast of performance at sdr funkball

roméo et juliette: roméo seul; grande fête chez capulets

turin 4 april 1960	rai torino orchestra	lp: cetra LAR 10 cd: cetra CDAR 2013 cd: curcio CON 11 cd: arkadia CD 437/CDMP 437

le carnaval romain, overture

munich 13 march 1989	munich po	cd: live classic best (japan) LCB 033/LCB 117
tokyo 16 october 1992	munich po	cd: gewandhaus music circle (japan) CG 22

les francs juges, overture

berlin 1951	berlin ro	lp: urania URLP 7024

GEORGES BIZET (1838-1875)

symphony in c

berlin	bpo	lp: cetra LO 533
9 november		cd: arkadia CD 734/CDGI 734
1953		cd: arlecchino ARL 157
		cd: nuova era NE 2301-2302
		all issues appear to be incorrectly dated

ALEXANDER BORODIN (1833-1887)

polovtsian dances

turin	rai torino	cd: arkadia CD 526/CDHP 526
9 january	orchestra	
1962		

JOHANNES BRAHMS (1833-1897)

symphony no 1

essen 29 september 1958	wdr orchestra	lp: paragon LBI 53007
rome 24 october 1958	wdr orchestra	cd: arkadia CD 764/CDGI 764 fourth movement only
milan 20 march 1959	rai milano orchestra	lp: cetra LAR 6 lp: movimento musica 04.002 cd: cetra CDAR 2009/CDO 120 cd: movimento musica 011.003/051.041 cd: arkadia CD 764/CDGI 764
mannheim 21 october 1976	sdr orchestra	cd: dg 459 6352/459 6362 also issued by audior in japan
stuttgart 11 february 1977	sdr orchestra	unpublished radio broadcast
london 13 april 1980	lso	cd: concert artists' recordings FED 004-006
munich 24 january 1981	munich po	cd: emi CDS 556 8372/CDS 556 8432 already issued by meteor and audior in japan
bucharest 14-16 february 1990	munich po	unpublished video recording of excerpts from rehearsal and performance

symphony no 2

milan 23-24 march 1959	rai milano orchestra	lp: cetra LAR 6 lp: movimento musica 04.002 cd: cetra CDAR 2010/CDO 120 cd: movimento musica 051.029/051.041 cd: arkadia CD 764/CDGI 764
turin 1960	rai torino orchestra	cd: legends LGD 109 cd: concert artists' recordings FED 004-006
stuttgart 11 april 1975	sdr orchestra	cd: dg 459 6352/459 6372 also 2 separate issues by audior in japan, one of which is dated 1980
munich 8 june 1991	munich po	cd: emi CDS 556 8372/CDS 556 8462 already issued by cincin and meteor in japan

symphony no 3

milan 20 march 1959	rai milano orchestra	lp: cetra LAR 6 lp: movimento musica 04.002 cd: cetra CDAR 2011/CDO 120 cd: movimento musica 051.029/051.041 cd: arkadia CD 764/CDGI 764
stuttgart 1960	sdr orchestra	cd: meteor (japan) MCD 043
paris 1974	orchestre national	cd: legends LGD 109 cd: concert artists' recordings FED 004-006
stuttgart 19 november 1976	sdr orchestra	cd: dg 459 6352/459 6372 also issued by audior in japan
munich 12 april 1987	munich po	cd: emi CDS 556 8372/CDS 556 8462

symphony no 4

berlin 18 november 1945	bpo	cd: myto MCD 981009 cd: tahra TAH 271 cd: grammofono AB 78774-78775
stuttgart 11 september 1958	sdr orchestra	cd: green hill (japan) GH 0017
milan 24 march 1959	rai milano orchestra	lp: cetra LAR 6 lp: movimento musica 04.002 cd: cetra CDAR 2011/CDO 120 cd: movimento musica 011.013/051.041 cd: arkadia CD 764/CDGI 764
berlin 14-15 january 1966	staatskapelle	cd: audior (japan) AUDSE 514-5I'5
wiesbaden 23 march 1974	sdr orchestra	lp: rococo 2150 cd: concert artists' recordings FED 004-006 cd: andromeda ANR 2507 cd: arlecchino ARLA 95 cd: dg 459 6352/459 6382 performance also issued by audior in japan
stuttgart 29 november 1974	sdr orchestra	cd: dg 459 6352/459 7452 rehearsal extracts
stuttgart 11 november 1982	sdr orchestra	cd: meteor (japan) MCD 048
munich 16 march 1985	munich po	cd: emi CDS 556 8372/CDC 556 8462 already issued on other labels in japan
tokyo 12 october 1990	munich po	cd: gewandhaus music circle (japan) CG 14

piano concerto no 1

munich 1987	munich po barenboim	cd: concert artists' recordings FED 048
erlangen 15-16 july 1991	munich po barenboim	vhs video: teldec 4509 990223 <u>third movement also issued on</u> <u>private cd by bayerischer rundfunk</u>

piano concerto no 2

munich november 1990	munich po barenboim	vhs video: teldec 4509 990223

violin concerto

berlin 21-22 september 1949	bpo menuhin	unpublished video recording of extracts from rehearsal and performance
london 5-6 march 1953	lso haendel	lp: hmv CLP 1032 cd: toshiba TOCE 8221-8222 cd: testament SBT 1038

alto rhapsody

turin 21 january 1959	rai torino and chorus höffgen	cd: arkadia CD 764/CDGI 764

ein deutsches requiem

rome 1954	rai roma orchestra and chorus seefried	cd: di stefano GDS 1206 ihr habt nun traurigkeit only
cologne 28 october 1957	wdr orchestra and chorus giebel, hotter	lp: discoreale DR 930058 cd: myto MCD 962147
milano 9 february 1960	rai milano orchestra and chorus giebel, prey	cd: arkadia CD 546/CDHP 546
munich 2 july 1981	munich po and chorus auger, gerihsen	cd: emi CDS 556 8372/CDS 556 8432

haydn variations

stuttgart 11 september 1959	sdr orchestra	unpublished radio broadcast
milan 29 january 1960	rai milano orchestra	cd: arkadia CD 445/CD 764/CDMP 445/ CDGI 764
milan 18 april 1969	rai milano orchestra	cd: exclusive EX92T 44-46
naples 12 november 1971	rai napoli orchestra	cd: cetra CDAR 2010/CDO 120
stuttgart 10 february 1977	sdr orchestra	cd: meteor (japan) MCD 048 incorrectly dated 1982; also issued by audior in japan

academic festival overture

stuttgart 23 february 1980	sdr orchestra	cd: audior (japan) AUDSE 510/ AUDSE 526-528

tragic overture

paris october 1974	orchestre national	cd: exclusive EX92T 52
stuttgart date not confirmed	sdr orchestra	cd: originals SH 841

hungarian dance no 1

stuttgart 29 november 1975	sdr orchestra	unpublished radio broadcast
mannheim 21 october 1976	sdr orchestra	unpublished radio broadcast
stuttgart 8 november 1979	sdr orchestra	unpublished radio broadcast of performance at sdr funkball
munich 1980	munich po	cd: audior (japan) AUDSE 508
stuttgart 10 june 1983	sdr orchestra	unpublished radio broadcast

CELIBIDACHE

Records for "His Master's Voice"

The first record to be made for "His Master's Voice" by this world-famous conductor is :

Prokofiev's "CLASSICAL" Symphony
with the
BERLIN PHILHARMONIC ORCHESTRA
C 3729-30

♪ **Music from today's Programme**

Overture, Hänsel and Gretel — *Humperdinck.* Hallé Orchestra, Conductor : Barbirolli   -   C 3623

'Pastoral Symphony' from The Messiah — *Handel.* London Symphony Orch. Cond. Sir Malcolm Sargent C2071

'Gayaneh' Ballet Suite : Dance of the Young Maidens, Sabre Dance, Lullaby — *Khachaturian.* Philharmonia Orch. Cond. Nicolai Malko -   -   - C 3572

Symphony No. 5 in E Minor — *Tchaikovsky.* London Philharmonic Orch. Cond. Constant Lambert C3088-92

"HIS MASTER'S VOICE"

The Hallmark of Quality

THE GRAMOPHONE COMPANY LIMITED, HAYES, MIDDLESEX

BENJAMIN BRITTEN (1913-1976)

sinfonia da requiem

berlin 10 november 1946	bpo	cd: tahra TAH 273

ANTON   BRUCKNER   (1824-1896)

symphony   no   3

stuttgart 25 november 1980	sdr orchestra	cd: exclusive EX93T 59 cd: dg awaiting publication <u>also issued on other cd labels in japan;</u> <u>EX93T 59 incorrectly dated 1981</u>
munich 16 october 1988	munich po	cd: emi CDC 556 6892/CDS 556 6882

symphony   no   4   "romantic"

stuttgart 9 november 1973	sdr orchestra	lp: rococo 2135 cd: arkadia CD 751/CDGI 751 cd: arlecchino ARL 175 cd: exclusive EX92T 23-24 cd: dg awaiting publication <u>also issued in japan by bells of</u> <u>sankt florian</u>
munich 19-20 march 1987	munich po	cd: emi CDC 556 6902/CDS 556 6882 <u>also issued in japan by meteor,</u> <u>although dated october 1988</u>
schleswig 13-15 august 1988	schleswig- holstein festival orchestra	vhs video: teldec 4509 964383 <u>rehearsal extracts only</u>
tokyo 15-24 april 1993	munich po	cd: gewandhaus music circle (japan) CG 20-21 <u>includes rehearsal extracts</u>

symphony no 5

stuttgart 25-26 november 1981	sdr orchestra	lp: sdr private issue cd: exclusive EX92T 44-46 cd: dg awaiting publication also issued in japan by bells of sankt florian
munich 10-11 november 1985	munich po	cd: audior (japan) AUDSE 523-524 also unpublished video recording; opening concert of gasteig concert hall
berlin 24 september 1986	munich po	cd: audior (japan) AUD 7007-7008
munich 14-16 february 1993	munich po	cd: emi CDC 556 6912/CDS 556 6882

symphony no 6

munich 26 november 1991	munich po	cd: concert artists' recordings FED 063 cd: emi CDC 556 6942/CDS 556 6882 vhs video: sony SHV 48348

symphony no 7

stuttgart 8 june 1971	sdr orchestra	cd: concert artists' recordings FED 011 cd: andromeda ANR 2513/NAS 2505 cd: arkadia CD 763/CDGI 763 cd: dg awaiting publication also issued in japan by partita and bells of sankt florian
munich 1985	munich po	cd: audior (japan) AUDM 2503-2504 also issued in japan by meteor
berlin 22 september 1989	munich po	cd: audior (japan) AUD 7009-7010
bucharest 15-17 february 1990	munich po	unpublished video recording of rehearsal extracts
tokyo 18 october 1990	munich po	vhs video: sony SHV 48316
berlin 31 march- 1 april 1992	bpo	vhs video: sony SHV 48352 celibidache's first concert with bpo after an interval of 38 years; issued on cd in japan by dumka and gewandhaus music circle; sony video includes rehearsal and documentary; sony video not yet published in all territories
munich 10 september 1994	munich po	cd: emi CDS 556 6952/CDS 556 6882

symphony no 8

stuttgart 17 december 1974	sdr orchestra	unpublished radio broadcast of rehearsal
stuttgart 20 december 1974	sdr orchestra	lp: rococo 2135 cd: exclusive EX92T 44-46 cd: dg awaiting publication <u>also issued by meteor in japan</u>
stuttgart 23 november 1976	sdr orchestra	unpublished radio broadcast
munich 4 april 1985	munich po	cd: audior (japan) AUDM 2505-2506 <u>also issued by meteor in japan</u>
tokyo 10 october 1990	munich po	cd: gewandhaus music circle (japan) CG 23-24
tokyo 20 october 1990	munich po	vhs video: sony SHV 48317
munich 12-13 september 1993	munich po	cd: emi CDS 556 6962/CDS 556 6882
lisbon 23 april 1994	munich po	cd: audior (japan) AUD 7001-7002

symphony no 9

turin 2 may 1969	rai torino orchestra	cd: cetra 9075.042 cd: arkadia CD 445/CDMP 445
stuttgart 5 april 1974	sdr orchestra	lp: rococo 2130 cd: arlecchino ARLA 14 cd: dg awaiting publication some editions were dated 1961
berlin 8 october 1981	munich po	cd: exclusive EX92T 23-24 also issued in japan by audior and meteor
munich march 1986	munich po	cd: audior (japan) AUDSE 520-521 also issued in japan by bells of sankt florian
munich 10 september 1995	munich po	cd: emi CDS 556 6992/CDS 556 6882 also includes rehearsal extracts recorded on 4-7 september 1995

te deum

| munich
1 july
1982 | munich po
and chorus
munich
bach choir
m.price, borchers,
ahnsjö, helm | cd: emi CDS 556 6952/CDS 556 6882 |

mass no 3

rome 15 march 1958	rai roma orchestra and chorus danco, höffgen, kmennt, guthrie	lp: melodram MEL 214
munich 6-13 september 1990	munich po and chorus m.price, soffel, straka, hölle/sotin	cd: exclusive EX92T 37-38 cd: emi CDC 556 7022/CDS 556 6882 <u>rehearsal extracts</u> vhs video: teldec 4509 964383
sankt florian 23 september 1990	munich po and chorus m.price, soffel, straka, sotin	unpublished video recording of performance and rehearsal extracts

FERRUCCIO BUSONI (1866-1924)

violin concerto

berlin 8 may 1949	bpo borries	cd: nuova era NE 6348-6349 cd: arkadia CD 734/CDGI 734

SERGIU CELIBIDACHE (1912-1996)

der taschengarten

stuttgart 21 may- 8 september 1979	sdr orchestra	lp: intercord INT 160.832 also issued on lp in japan by philips

LUIGI CHERUBINI (1760-1842)

symphony in d

venice 31 october 1965	la fenice orchestra	cd: originals SH 857

anacréon overture

stuttgart 8 march 1974	sdr orchestra	lp: rococo 2150 cd: audior (japan) AUDSE 510

FREDERIC CHOPIN (1810-1849)

piano concerto no 2

berlin	berlin ro	lp: rococo 2095
25 october	koczalski	lp: replica RPL 2462
1948		

AARON COPLAND (1900-1990)

appalachian spring

berlin	bpo	cd: gewandhaus music circle (japan)
6 april		CG 26-27
1950		

ARCANGELO CORELLI (1653-1713)

christmas concerto in g minor

naples 7 december 1959	rai napoli orchestra	cd: originals SH 864
milan 22 february 1960	rai milano orchestra	lp: cetra LAR 22

LUIGI DALLAPICCOLA (1904-1975)

partita for soprano and orchestra

turin 20 july 1968	rai torino orchestra rizzoli	cd: stradivarius STR 13608

CLAUDE DEBUSSY (1862-1918)

la mer

milan 29 january 1960	rai milano orchestra	lp: cetra LAR 38 cd: nuova era NE 2204/NE 2393-2398 cd: cetra CDAR 2058 cd: arkadia CD 485/CDMP 485
copenhagen 1970	danish ro	cd: originals SH 860
paris 1974	orchestre national	cd: live classic best (japan) LCB 078/LCB 139
stuttgart 11 february 1977	sdr orchestra	lp: rococo 2155 cd: concert artists' recordings FED 031 cd: dg awaiting publication
munich 27 september 1991	munich po	cd: meteor (japan) MCD 033
munich 13 september 1992	munich po	cd: emi CDC 556 5202/CDS 556 5172

3 nocturnes

stuttgart 17 october 1978 and 15 november 1980	sdr orchestra and chorus	lp: rococo 2155 cd: dg awaiting publication 1978 performance was also an unpublished video recording

jeux

berlin 20 march 1948	bpo	cd: arlecchino ARL 157 cd: arkadia CD 734/CDGI 734 cd: nuova era NE 6348-6349 cd: grammofono AB 78774-78775

prélude a l'apres-midi d'un faune

stuttgart 28 november 1975	sdr orchestra	lp: rococo 2155 cd: audior (japan) AUD 7004
london 18 september 1979	lso	cd: concert artists' recordings FED 031 cd: exclusive EX95T 82 also issued in japan by campanella and live classic best

petite suite

berlin 5 may 1949	berlin ro	lp: varese VC 81110 cd: arlecchino ARL 157

ibéria/images

stuttgart 29 february 1980	sdr orchestra	cd: dg awaiting publication
london 10 april 1980	lso	cd: concert artists' recordings FED 031 also issued in japan by live classic best
munich 22 september 1992	munich po	cd: emi CDC 556 5202/CDS 556 5172

la demoiselle élue

turin 30 january 1959	rai torino orchestra and chorus sautereau, fioroni	lp: rococo 2155 lp: cetra LAR 38 cd: cetra CDAR 2058 cd: arlecchino ARLA 87

PAUL DUKAS (1865-1935)

l'apprenti sorcier

london   lso   cd: galileo (japan) GL 9
8 april
1982

ANTONIN DVORAK (1841-1904)

symphony no 7

munich 1987	munich po	cd: concert artists' recordings FED 040

symphony no 9 "from the new world"

turin 5 january 1962	rai torino orchestra	cd: frequenz 041.010 cd: curcio CON 04 cd: bella musica BMF 968 cd: arkadia CD 526/CDHP 526
stuttgart 17 october 1978	sdr orchestra	lp: rococo 2163 cd: arlecchino ARL 165 also issued in japan by audior and meteor
munich 16 june 1985	munich po	cd: meteor (japan) MCD 034 also issued on other labels in japan
munich october 1991	munich po	vhs video: teldec 4509 964383 excerpts vhs video: teldec 4509 957103

cello concerto

berlin 1945	berlin ro fournier	cd: pearl GEMMCD 9198 cd: grammofono AB 78730 <u>AB 78730 incorrectly describes orchestra as london philharmonic</u>
paris 3-5 october 1974	orchestre national fournier	cd: arkadia CD 615/CDHP 615 cd: arlecchino ARL 165 <u>also unpublished video recording</u>
munich november 1987	munich po schiff	cd: audior (japan) AUDSE 502

slavonic dance no 1

stuttgart 5 june 1965	sdr orchestra	unpublished radio broadcast
copenhagen 1970	danish ro	cd: documents LV 965
turin 1970	rai torino orchestra	cd: arkadia CD 615/CDHP 615
turin 20 june 1975	rai torino orchestra	cd: live classic best (japan) LCB 013/LCB 107
stuttgart 28 november 1975	sdr orchestra	unpublished radio broadcast
mannheim 21 october 1976	sdr orchestra	unpublished radio broadcast
stuttgart 10 june 1983	sdr orchestra	unpublished radio broadcast of performance at sdr funkball

slavonic dance no 2

copenhagen 1970	danish ro	cd: documents LV 965
turin 1970	rai torino orchestra	cd: arkadia CD 615/CDHP 615
turin 20 june 1975	rai torino orchestra	cd: live classic best (japan) LCB 013/LCB 107
stuttgart 9 june 1982	sdr orchestra	unpublished radio broadcast of performance at sdr funkball

slavonic dance no 3

copenhagen 1970	danish ro	cd: documents LV 965
turin 1970	rai torino orchestra	cd: arkadia CD 615/CDHP 615

slavonic dance no 4

| turin
1970 | rai torino
orchestra | cd: arkadia CD 615/CDHP 615 |

slavonic dance no 5

copenhagen 1970	danish ro	cd: documents LV 965
turin 1970	rai torino orchestra	cd: arkadia CD 615/CDHP 615
turin 20 june 1975	rai torino orchestra	cd: live classic best (japan) LCB 013/LCB 107

slavonic dance no 6

| copenhagen
1970 | danish ro | cd: documents LV 965 |
| turin
1970 | rai torino
orchestra | cd: arkadia CD 615/CDHP 615 |

slavonic dance no 7

copenhagen 1970	danish ro	cd: documents LV 965
turin 1970	rai torino orchestra	cd: arkadia CD 615/CDHP 615

slavonic dance no 8

stuttgart 5 june 1965	sdr orchestra	unpublished radio broadcast
berlin 14-15 january 1966	staatskapelle	cd: audior (japan) AUDSE 514-515
copenhagen 1970	danish ro	cd: documents LV 965
turin 1970	rai torino orchestra	cd: arkadia CD 615/CDHP 615
turin 20 june 1975	rai torino orchestra	cd: live classic best (japan) LCB 013/LCB 107
stuttgart 22 june 1976	sdr orchestra	unpublished radio broadcast
munich 1980	munich po	cd: audior (japan) AUDSE 508
munich 14 october 1986	munich po	cd: gewandhaus music circle (japan) CG 17

MANUEL DE FALLA (1876-1946)

miller's dance/el sombrero de 3 picos

stuttgart 22 june 1976	sdr orchestra	unpublished radio broadcast

GABRIEL FAURE (1845-1924)

requiem

london 8 april 1982	lso lso chorus mclaughlin, howell	cd: exclusive EX92T 52 cd: arlecchino ARLA 87 also issued by campanella and live classic best in japan; also unpublished video recording of rehearsal extract

CESAR FRANCK (1822-1890)

symphony in d minor

turin 12 january 1962	rai torino orchestra	cd: arkadia CD 750/CDGI 750
stuttgart 27-28 february 1982	sdr orchestra	cd: concert artists' recordings FED 034 also issued in japan by audior
munich october- november 1991	munich po	cd: audior (japan) AUDSE 506

variations symphoniques pour piano et orchestre

location and date not confirmed	orchestra sonoda	lp: rococo 2136

GIROLAMO FRESCOBALDI (1583-1643)

ricerare e toccata, arranged by celibidache

naples	rai napoli	cd: foyer CDS 17001
22 october	orchestra	
1961		

ANDREA GABRIELI (1510-1586)

aria della battaglia, arranged by ghedini

turin	rai torino	lp: cetra LAR 32
8 april	orchestra	
1960		
stuttgart	sdr orchestra	cd: green hill (japan) GH 0017
22 january		
1964		

REINHOLD GLIERE (1875-1956)

concerto for coloratura soprano and orchestra

berlin	bpo	cd: myto MCD 981009
6-7	berger	cd: grammofono AB 78774-78775
july		
1946		

EDVARD GRIEG (1843-1907)

piano concerto

stuttgart 23 november 1972	sdr orchestra michelangeli	cd: arlecchino ARLA 06 incorrectly dated 28 october 1973

GEORGE FRIDERIC HANDEL (1685-1759)

concerto grosso op 6 no 1

munich 22 june 1991	munich po	cd: audior (japan) AUD 7012

FRANZ JOSEF HAYDN (1732-1809)

symphony no 92 "oxford"

munich 28 february 1993	munich po	cd: emi CDC 556 5192/CDS 556 5172
tokyo 28 april 1993	munich po	cd: gewandhaus music circle (japan) CG 17

symphony no 94 "surprise"

berlin 28 september 1946	bpo	cd: tahra TAH 273 cd: grammofono AB 78774-78775
nürnberg 20 november 1973	sdr orchestra	unpublished radio broadcast

symphony no 102

stuttgart 17 september 1959	sdr orchestra	lp: rococo 2140 cd: arlecchino ARLA 92

symphony no 103 "drum roll"

stuttgart 8 march 1974	sdr orchestra	cd: originals SH 808 cd: arlecchino ARLA 92 incorrectly dated 26 september 1971; also issued in japan by audior
munich 11-12 november 1993	munich po	cd: emi CDC 556 5182/CDS 556 5172

symphony no 104 "london"

berlin 20 february 1950	bpo	lp: cetra LO 533 cd: arkadia CD 734/CDGI 734 cd: curcio CON 23 cd: arlecchino ARLA 96 cd: nuova era NE 6348-6349
stuttgart 25 november 1980	sdr orchestra	cd: audior (japan) AUD 7013
munich 14 april 1992	munich po	cd: emi CDC 556 5182/CDS 556 5172

trumpet concerto

munich 22 june 1991	munich po komischke	cd: audior (japan) AUD 7012

PAUL HINDEMITH (1895-1963)

mathis der maler, symphony

copenhagen 3 october 1968	danish ro	cd: arlecchino ARL 172
stuttgart 8 june 1971	sdr orchestra	cd: meteor (japan) MCD 050-051
berlin 8 october 1981	munich po	cd: exclusive EX92T 37-38 also issued in japan by meteor

philharmonisches konzert

stuttgart 9 december 1976	sdr orchestra	unpublished radio broadcast

piano concerto

berlin 4 september 1949	bpo puchelt	cd: nuova era NE 6348-6349 german premiere performance

cello concerto

stuttgart 2 april 1976	sdr orchestra böttcher	unpublished radio broadcast

der schwanendreher, for viola and orchestra

location and date not confirmed	orchestra giuranna	lp: rococo 2165

symphonic metamorphoses on themes of carl maria von weber

berlin 1950	bpo	cd: gewandhaus music circle (japan) CG 26-27
stuttgart 11 september 1958	sdr orchestra	unpublished radio broadcast
stuttgart 22 october 1964	sdr orchestra	unpublished radio broadcast
berlin 14-15 january 1966	staatskapelle	cd: audior (japan) AUDSE 514-516
cologne 1970	wdr orchestra	lp: rococo 2165 cd: live classic best (japan) LCB 085/LCB 143

kammermusik no 2

naples 15 december 1959	rai napoli orchestra gorini	cd: originals SH 864

ZOLTAN KODALY (1882-1967)

dances of galanta

stuttgart date not confirmed	sdr orchestra	cd: arlecchino ARLA 97
london 13 april 1980	lso	cd: concert artists' recordings FED 053
osaka 26 april 1980	lso	cd: gewandhaus music circle (japan) CG 22

FRANZ LISZT (1811-1886)

les préludes

vienna 30 october 1952	vienna so	cd: nuova era NE 2291/NE 2393-2398

GUSTAV MAHLER (1860-1911)

kindertotenlieder

munich 30 june 1983	munich po fassbaender	cd: topazio (japan) TP 26049

GIAN FRANCESCO MALIPIERO (1882-1973)

symphony no 4

location and date not confirmed	orchestra	lp: rococo 2156

MARGOLA

partita for string orchestra

naples 5 january 1959	rai napoli orchestra	cd: originals SH 864

FELIX   MENDELSSOHN-BARTHOLDY   (1809-1847)

symphony   no   4   "italian"

berlin 9 november 1953	bpo	lp: cetra LO 533 lp: movimento musica 01.031 lp: fabbri GCL 10 cd: arkadia CD 734/CDGI 734 cd: curcio CON 02 cd: arlecchino ARLA 96 cd: frequenz 041.010 cd: nuova era NE 6348-6349 some editions incorrectly dated 1950
munich 1993	munich po	cd: ca d'oro CO 93516

violin   concerto

berlin 1949-1950	bpo borries	lp: toshiba EAB 5002 cd: toshiba TOCE 8221-8222
munich 1993	munich po krstic	cd: ca d'oro CO 93516

the hebrides, overture

stuttgart 9 december 1976	sdr orchestra	lp: rococo 2136 cd: originals SH 841 also issued by topazio in japan

a midsummer night's dream, overture

stuttgart 30 november 1980	sdr orchestra	cd: concert artists' recordings FED 048 cd: arlecchino ARLA 95 also issued by audior in japan; also unpublished video recording

die schöne melusine, overture

berlin august 1945	berlin ro	cd: tahra TAH 273

DARIUS MILHAUD (1892-1974)

saudades do brasil

naples 8 february 1957	rai napoli orchestra	lp: cetra LAR 38 cd: cetra CDAR 2058
stuttgart 31 october 1979	sdr orchestra	unpublished radio broadcast

suite française

munich september- october 1991	munich po	cd: audior (japan) AUDSE 509

WOLFGANG AMADEUS MOZART (1756-1791)

symphony no 25

london	lpo	78: london (usa) LA 97
9 april-		lp: decca LXT 2558/ECM 836
29 december		lp: london (usa) LLP 88
1948		

symphony no 35 "haffner"

stuttgart	sdr orchestra	unpublished radio broadcast
20 june		
1976		

munich	munich po	cd: galileo (japan) GL 2
22 june		also issued by audior in japan
1991		

symphony no 38 "prague"

stuttgart	sdr orchestra	cd: originals SH 808
28 march		
1974		

symphony no 39

stuttgart	sdr orchestra	cd: arlecchino ARL 187
29 november		incorrectly dated 13 may 1972
1974		

munich	munich po	cd: audior (japan) AUD 7006
1991		

symphony no 40

stuttgart 27 november 1973	sdr orchestra	cd: arlecchino ARL 187 cd: documents LV 907-908 also issued in japan by meteor
stuttgart 28 february 1982	sdr orchestra	cd: exclusive EX92T 28
munich 3 june 1983	munich po	cd: cincin CCCD 1008
munich 15 march 1994	munich po	cd: emi CDC 556 5192/CDS 556 5172

symphony no 41 "jupiter"

stuttgart 8 november 1979	sdr orchestra	unpublished radio broadcast

piano concerto no 9

munich 16 january 1996	munich po perahia	cd: audior (japan) AUDSE 507

concerto for 2 pianos and orchestra

rome 11 may 1968	rai roma orchestra bruno aprea, tito aprea	cd: cetra CDAR 2017/CDE 1059/ CDO 128

violin concerto no 5

berlin 6 march 1950	bpo d'albore	cd: arkadia CD 734/CDGI 734 cd: arlecchino ARLA 93
stuttgart 29 november 1973	sdr orchestra rogoff	unpublished radio broadcast

flute concerto no 2

turin 21 march 1958	rai torino gazzelloni	lp: sarpe 7009 lp: rococo 2140 cd: curcio CON 027 cd: memories HR 4125 cd: sarpe 7009
stuttgart 3 february 1968	sdr orchestra gazzelloni	cd: arlecchino ARL 187

sinfonia concertante for violin and viola

munich 9 february 1990	munich po krstic, nicolai	cd: audior (japan) AUD 7012

serenade no 7 "haffner"

naples 22 april 1968	rai napoli orchestra	lp: sarpe 7005 cd: cetra CDAR 2017/CDE 1059/ CDO 128

serenade no 13 "eine kleine nachtmusik"

| naples 7 december 1959 | rai napoli orchestra | cd: originals SH 864 |

ländler k606

| milan 22 february 1960 | rai milano orchestra | lp: cetra LAR 22 cd: documents LV 907-908 cd: nuova era NE 2291/NE 2393-2398 |

| munich february 1991 | munich po | cd: audior (japan) AUDSE 505 also issued in japan by partita |

don giovanni, overture

| munich 29 november 1989 | munich po | cd: audior (japan) AUD 7006 |

mass in c minor "great"

| rome 26 march 1960 | rai roma orchestra and chorus giebel, lear, munteanu, guthrie | lp: cetra LAR 1 cd: cetra CDAR 2007/CDO 128 cd: arkadia CD 424/CDMP 424 cd: curcio CON 34 excerpts cd: cetra CDPR 1001 |

| stuttgart 30 november 1973 | sdr orchestra sdr and bavarian radio choruses auger, harper, laubenthal, cold | cd: audior (japan) AUD 7005 also issued in japan by topazio |

requiem

milan 16 march 1962	rai milano orchestra and chorus giebel, höffgen, traxel, arié	cd: arkadia CD 425/CDMP 425
turin 3 may 1968	rai torino orchestra and chorus putz, hamari, gricknick, schramm	lp: rococo 2152 cd: curcio CON 10 cd: documents LV 907-908 cd: nuova era NE 2393-2398
munich 16-17 april 1987	munich po and chorus venuti, kunz, heilmann, lika	cd: concert artists' recordings FED 039

MODEST MUSSORGSKY (1839-1881)

pictures from an exhibition, arranged by ravel

turin 30 january 1959	rai torino orchestra	cd: arkadia CD 436/CDMP 436
venice 31 october 1965	la fenice orchestra	cd: originals SH 857
stuttgart 21-22 june 1976	sdr orchestra	cd: dg awaiting publication
berlin 23 september 1986	munich po	cd: concert artists' recordings FED 017 also issued in japan by audior
chicago 16 april 1989	munich po	cd: concert artists' recordings FED 068
ingolstadt 16 september 1989	munich po	unpublished video recording
munich 24-25 september 1993	munich po	cd: emi CDC 556 5262/CDC 556 5292/ CDS 556 5172

another version of the work with munich po appears in japan on the
meteor and audior labels

night on bald mountain

milan 1967	rai milano orchestra	cd: concert artists' recordings FED 017 cd: originals SH 841

CARL NIELSEN (1865-1931)

maskarade, overture

| stuttgart
5 june
1965 | sdr orchestra | unpublished radio broadcast |

CARL ORFF (1895-1982)

carmina burana

| munich
10 november
1985 | munich po
and chorus | unpublished video recording |

HANS PFITZNER (1869-1949)

palestrina, act 2 prelude

| munich
10 november
1985 | munich po | unpublished video recording |

SERGEY PROKOFIEV (1891-1953)

symphony no 1 "classical"

berlin 4-6 february 1948	bpo	78: hmv C 3729-3730 lp: victor LBC 1009 lp: emi RLS 768/F 669.711-669.715 lp: rococo 2082 cd: nuova era NE 2301-2302 cd: emi CDF 300 1222/CZS 569 7432 third movement cd: emi CMS 566 1822
munich march 1988	munich po	vhs video: teldec 9031 736673 includes rehearsal extracts

symphony no 5

stuttgart 11 september 1959	sdr orchestra	unpublished radio broadcast
milan 29 january 1960	rai milano orchestra	lp: cetra LAR 15 cd: arkadia CD 434/CDMP 434 cd: nuova era NE 2204/NE 2393-2398
turin 30 april 1970	rai torino orchestra	cd: cetra CDAR 2016
stuttgart 31 october 1979	sdr orchestra	cd: dg awaiting publication
munich 23 february 1990	munich po	cd: meteor (japan) MCD 045

MAURICE RAVEL (1875-1937)

piano concerto in g

stuttgart 19 december 1975	sdr orchestra zacharias	unpublished radio broadcast
london 8 april 1982	lso michelangeli	cd: arlecchino ARLA 79 cd: exclusive EX92T 61-62 also unpublished video recording
munich 5 june 1992	munich po michelangeli	cd: galileo (japan) GL 02

piano concerto for the left hand

vienna 30 october 1952	vienna so casadesus	cd: documents LV 946-947 cd: nuova era NE 2318/NE 2393-2398 cd: arlecchino ARLA 79 ARLA 79 incorrectly describes orchestra as vienna philharmonic

pavane pour une infante défunte

turin 10 april 1970	rai torino orchestra	cd: cetra CDAR 2008/CDO 136

alborada del gracioso

turin 30 january 1959	rai torino orchestra	lp: cetra LAR 38 cd: cetra CDAR 2060 cd: arkadia CD 741/CDGI 741 cd: nuova era NE 2318/NE 2393-2398
stuttgart 11 november 1959	sdr orchestra	unpublished radio broadcast
stockholm date not confirmed	swedish ro	cd: gewandhaus music circle (japan) CG 28
nürnberg 20 november 1973	sdr orchestra	cd: dg awaiting publication
paris 4 june 1974	orchestre national	cd: exclusive EX92T 61-62 cd: documents LV 946-947 cd: originals SH 841 cd: arlecchino ARLA 78 also issued in japan by campanella and live classic best
stuttgart 4 november 1982	sdr orchestra	unpublished video recording

boléro

turin 14 may 1954	rai torino orchestra	lp: cetra LAR 38 cd: cetra CDAR 2060 cd: nuova era NE 2318/NE 2393-2398
milan 11 february 1966	rai milano orchestra	cd: arkadia CD 741/CDGI 741
stuttgart 11 april 1975	sdr orchestra	cd: documents LV 946-947 also issued in japan by topazio

piano concerto no 3

turin	rai torino	cd: arkadia CD 405/CDMP 405
5 january	orchestra	
1962	weissenberg	

piano concerto no 5

milan	rai milano	cd: cetra CDAR 2016/CDE 1029
17 february	orchestra	
1967	perticaroli	

violin concerto no 1

naples	rai napoli	cd: arkadia CD 434/CDMP 434
22 december	orchestra	cd: nuova era NE 2335
1957	gulli	

romeo and juliet, excerpts from the ballet

turin 4 april 1960	rai torino orchestra	lp: cetra LAR 10 cd: cetra CDAR 2013 cd: nuova era NE 2291/NE 2393-2398 cd: arkadia CD 434/CDMP 434 <u>excerpts</u> cd: cetra CDPR 1001
paris 1974	orchestre national	cd: campanella (japan) 002 <u>also issued in japan by live classic best</u>
stuttgart 12-13 february 1981	sdr orchestra	cd: concert artists' recordings FED 055 <u>also issued in japan by audior</u>

scythian suite

berlin 14-15 january 1966	staatskapelle	lp: rococo 2136 cd: audior (japan) AUDSE 514-515
stuttgart 27-28 november 1975	sdr orchestra	cd: dg awaiting publication

daphnis et chloé, first suite

milan 17 april 1970	rai milano orchestra	cd: cetra CDAR 2008/CDO 136 cd: arkadia CD 485/CDMP 485
munich date not confirmed	munich po	cd: arlecchino ARLA 79 cd: andromeda NAS 2501 cd: originals SH 803
munich 21-22 june 1987	munich po	cd: audior (japan) AUDSE 509

daphnis et chloé, second suite

milan 17 april 1970	rai milano orchestra and chorus	cd: cetra CDAR 2008/CDO 136 cd: arkadia CD 485/CDMP 485
paris 1974	orchestre national	cd: documents LV 946-947 cd: exclusive EX92T 61-62
munich date not confirmed	munich po	cd: arlecchino ARLA 79 cd: andromeda NAS 2501 cd: originals SH 803
stuttgart 1974	sdr orchestra	cd: dg awaiting publication already issued in japan by meteor
munich 21-22 june 1987	munich po and chorus	cd: audior AUDSE 509 also issued in japan by live classic best, but dated 1985; also unpublished video recording

ma mere l'oye

milan 22 january 1960	rai milano orchestra	lp: cetra LAR 38 lp: fabbri GCL 22 cd: arkadia CD 741/CDGI 741 cd: cetra CDAR 2060 cd: nuova era NE 2318/NE 2393-2398
stuttgart 1972	sdr orchestra	cd: arlecchino ARLA 78 cd: documents LV 946-947 also unpublished video recording of rehearsal extracts
london 13 april 1980	lso	cd: exclusive EX92T 61-62
osaka 26 april 1980	lso	cd: gewandhaus music circle (japan) CG 18

rapsodie espagnole

viernes 7 december 1962	caracas so	cd: arkadia CD 741/CDGI 741
stuttgart date not confirmed	sdr orchestra	cd: dg awaiting publication
london 18 september 1979	lso	cd: arlecchino ARLA 78 cd: documents LV 946-947 cd: exclusive EX92T 61-62 also issued in japan by live classic best
munich october 1980	munich po	cd: meteor (japan) MCD 027 also unpublished video recording of rehearsal extract

le tombeau de couperin

naples 17 december 1957	rai napoli orchestra	lp: cetra LAR 38 cd: cetra CDAR 2060 cd: arkadia CD 741/CDGI 741 cd: nuova era NE 2318/NE 2393-2398
copenhagen 3 october 1968	danish ro	cd: arlecchino ARL 172
paris 1974	orchestre national	cd: documents LV 946-947
tübingen 26 october 1978	sdr orchestra	cd: arlecchino ARLA 78 cd: exclusive EX92T 61-62 cd: dg awaiting publication
munich january 1989	munich po	cd: meteor (japan) MCD 027

the lp rococo 2155 contains either the copenhagen, paris or stuttgart performances

la valse

milan 18 april 1969	rai milano orchestra	cd: cetra CDAR 2008/CDO 136 cd: exclusive EX92T 61-62 cd: documents LV 946-947 cd: arkadia CD 485/CDMP 485
paris 1976	orchestre national	cd: live classic best (japan) LCB 077/LCB 139
stuttgart 19 november 1976	sdr orchestra	cd: dg awaiting publication
munich 20 january 1980	munich po	cd: kyoun (japan) SCD 629-630

assez lent/valses nobles et sentimentales

stuttgart 10 april 1975	sdr orchestra	unpublished radio broadcast
mannheim 21 october 1976	sdr orchestra	unpublished radio broadcast

OTTORINO RESPIGHI (1879-1936)

pini di roma

turin 1 april 1960	rai torino orchestra	lp: cetra LAR 32 cd: nuova era NE 2238 nuova era incorrectly dated 1968
stuttgart 23 november 1972	sdr orchestra	cd: originals SH 860
paris 13 december 1974	orchestre national	cd: concert artists' recordings FED 034 cd: arkadia CD 487/CDMP 487
stuttgart 20 june 1976	sdr orchestra	cd: dg awaiting publication

NIKOLAI RIMSKY-KORSAKOV (1844-1908)

scheherazade

turin 24 february 1967	rai torino orchestra	lp: rococo 2154 cd: curcio CON 15 cd: arkadia CD 436/CDMP 436
stuttgart 29 february 1980	sdr orchestra	cd: arlecchino ARL 126 cd: originals SH 889 also issued in japan by audior and live classic best; most editions appear to be incorrectly dated
munich 1980	munich po	cd: exclusive EX95T 82 also issued in japan by meteor
stuttgart 18 february 1982	sdr orchestra	unpublished video recording

GIOACHINO ROSSINI (1792-1868)

la gazza ladra, overture

stuttgart 29 february 1980	sdr orchestra	cd: gewandhaus music circle (japan) CG 25
munich date not confirmed	munich po	cd: audior (japan) AUDSE 508
tokyo 12 october 1990	munich po	cd: gewandhaus music circle (japan) CG 15

semiramide, overture

munich june 1992	munich po	cd: galileo (japan) GL 02

ALBERT ROUSSEL (1869-1937)

petite suite pour orchestre

berlin 24 july 1945	bpo	cd: tahra TAH 273
berlin 5 may 1949	berlin ro	lp: varese VC 81110 cd: arlecchino ARL 157

CAMILLE SAINT-SAENS (1835-1921)

introduction and rondo capriccioso

stockholm	swedish ro	cd: gewandhaus music circle (japan)
date not	haendel	CG 28
confirmed		

samson et dalila, excerpt (mon coeur s'ouvre a ta voix)

berlin	bpo	lp: eterna 820 922
20 january	klose	cd: tahra TAH 273
1946	<u>sung in german</u>	

ARNOLD SCHOENBERG (1874-1951)

variations for orchestra

lucerne	swiss festival	cd: gewandhaus music circle (japan)
14 august	orchestra	CG 28
1974		

FRANZ SCHUBERT (1797-1828)

symphony no 2

cologne 5 october 1958	wdr orchestra	lp: fabbri GCL 10 lp: movimento musica 01.027

symphony no 5

turin 24 april 1970	rai torino orchestra	cd: cetra CDAR 2014/CDO 124/ 9075.047
stuttgart 9 november 1973	sdr orchestra	cd: memories HR 4190
paris 30 december 1973	orchestre national	cd: arkadia CD 489/CDMP 489

symphony no 6

lucerne 14 august 1974	swiss festival orchestra	cd: gewandhaus music circle (japan) CG 28

symphony no 8 "unfinished"

rome 11 march 1958	rai roma orchestra	cd: arkadia CD 548/CDHP 548
lugano 14 june 1963	swiss-italian radio orchestra	cd: ermitage ERM 114/120 032
turin 24 april 1970	rai torino orchestra	cd: cetra CDAR 2014/CDO 124/ 9075.047
munich september 1988	munich po	cd: meteor (japan) MCD 020-021
tokyo 26 april 1993	munich po	cd: gewandhaus music circle (japan) CG 19
tokyo 30 april 1993	munich po	cd: gewandhaus music circle (japan) CG 17

symphony no 9 "great"

rome 24 november 1961	rai roma orchestra	cd: arkadia CD 548/CDHP 548
stuttgart 2 april 1976	sdr orchestra	unpublished radio broadcast
stuttgart 31 october 1979	sdr orchestra	unpublished radio broadcast
munich 28 february 1994	munich po	cd: emi CDC 556 5272/CDS 556 5172 it is not clear if a performance of the symphony issued in japan by meteor and audior is this one or another

rosamunde, overture

milan 1960	rai milano orchestra	cd: arkadia CD 489/CDMP 489

rosamunde, entr'acte no 3

munich february 1991	munich po	cd: partita (japan) PC 9102 also issued in japan by audior

6 german dances, arranged by webern

milan 22 february 1960	rai milano orchestra	lp: rococo 2132 lp: cetra LAR 22 cd: nuova era NE 2291/NE 2393-2398
stuttgart 22 october 1964	sdr orchestra	unpublished radio broadcast
stuttgart 28 november 1975	sdr orchestra	unpublished radio broadcast this recording contains only dances nos 5 and 6
munich february 1991	munich po	cd: partita (japan) PC 9102 also issued in japan by audior

ROBERT SCHUMANN (1810-1856)

symphony no 1 "spring"

stuttgart june 1963	sdr orchestra	lp: rococo 2132 cd: arlecchino ARL 191

milan
5 april
1968
	rai milano
	orchestra
		cd: cetra CDAR 2015/CD0 124/
		   CDE 1058
		cd: concert artists' recordings
		   FED 009-010

stuttgart 13 february 1981	sdr orchestra	cd: audior (japan) AUDSE 517

symphony no 2

rome 18 march 1960	rai roma orchestra	lp: cetra LAR 14 cd: arkadia CD 413/CDMP 413 cd: nuova era NE 2367/NE 2393-2398
viersen 7 november 1961	royal danish orchestra	lp: movimento musica 01.022 cd: arlecchino ARL 191
stockholm 1969	swedish ro	lp: rococo 2139 cd: arkadia CD 737/CDGI 737
rome 12 april 1969	rai roma orchestra	cd: cetra CDAR 2015/CDO 124/ CDE 1058/9075.052
tübingen 26 october 1978	sdr orchestra	unpublished radio broadcast
london 12 september 1979	lso	cd: concert artists' recordings FED 009-010

symphony no 3 "rhenish"

munich 21 april 1988	munich po	cd: arlecchino ARLA 94 cd: concert artists' recordings FED 009-010 cd: emi CDC 556 5252/CDS 556 5172

symphony no 4

nürnberg 20 november 1973	sdr orchestra	unpublished radio broadcast
munich 20 september 1986	munich po	cd: arlecchino ARLA 94 cd: emi CD 556 5252/CDS 556 5172 also issued in japan by audior
berlin 23 september 1986	munich po	cd: concert artists' recordings FED 009-010 also issued in japan by audior
yokahama 13 october 1986	munich po	cd: gewandhaus music circle (japan) CG 23-24

piano concerto

stockholm 19 november 1967	swedish ro michelangeli	cd: arkadia CD 592/CDHP 592/LE 951
paris 4 june 1974	orchestre national argerich	cd: concert artists' recordings FED 012 also issued in japan by campanella
erlangen 15-16 july 1991	munich po barenboim	vhs video: teldec 4509 941923
tokyo 16 october 1992	munich po michelangeli	cd: concert artists' recordings FED 027 also issued in japan by gewandhaus music circle

DMITRI SHOSTAKOVICH (1906-1975)

symphony no 1

copenhagen 1973	danish ro	cd: originals SH 863

symphony no 5

turin 21 february 1955	rai torino orchestra	cd: arkadia CD 765/CDGI 765
munich 6 february 1986	munich po	cd: partita (japan) PC 9106

symphony no 7 "leningrad"

berlin 22 december 1946	bpo	lp: urania URLP 601 cd: arlecchino ARL 106 cd: theorema TH 121.122 cd: grammofono AB 78685 also unpublished video recording of excerpt from this german premiere performance

symphony no 9

milan 17 february 1967	rai milano orchestra	cd: arkadia CD 765/CDGI 765
munich 9 february 1990	munich po	cd: audior (japan) AUDES 520-521 also issued in japan by meteor

JEAN SIBELIUS (1865-1957)

symphony no 2

lucerne 14 august 1974	swiss festival orchestra	lp: rococo 2131 cd: audior (japan) AUD 7014

symphony no 5

turin 10 april 1970	rai torino orchestra	cd: arkadia CD 616/CDHP 616
copenhagen 7 october 1971	danish ro	cd: originals SH 863

violin concerto

milan 1969	rai milano orchestra haendel	cd: nuova era NE 2335

en saga

helsinki 20 may 1969	swedish ro	cd: arkadia CD 616/CDHP 616
london 21 september 1979	lso	cd: concert artists' recordings FED 055
stuttgart 12 november 1981	sdr orchestra	unpublished radio broadcast

valse triste

milan 22 february 1960	rai milano	lp: cetra LAR 22 cd: arkadia CD 616/CDHP 616 cd: nuova era NE 2291/NE 2393-2398

BEDRICH SMETANA (1824-1884)

the moldau/ma vlast

munich 20-21 june 1986	munich po	cd: kyoun (japan) SCD 629-630

RUDI STEPHAN (1887-1915)

musik für orchester

stuttgart 23 february 1980	sdr orchestra	unpublished radio broadcast

JOHANN AND JOSEF STRAUSS

pizzicato polka

stuttgart 27 may 1981	sdr orchestra	unpublished radio broadcast of performance at sdr funkball
munich date not confirmed	munich po	cd: audior (japan) AUDSE 508

JOHANN STRAUSS II (1825-1899)

annen polka

stuttgart 27 may 1981	sdr orchestra	unpublished radio broadcast of performance at sdr funkball

auf der jagd, polka

stuttgart 10 june 1983	sdr orchestra	unpublished radio broadcast of performance at sdr funkball

die fledermaus, overture

paris 1973	orchestre national	cd: concert artists' recordings FED 040
stuttgart 27 may 1981	sdr orchestra	unpublished radio broadcast of performance at sdr funkball
munich february 1991	munich po	cd: audior (japan) AUDSE 505 also issued in japan by partita

g'schichten aus dem wienerwald, waltz

paris 1973	orchestre national	cd: concert artists' recordings FED 040

kaiser-walzer

| stuttgart 27 may 1981 | sdr orchestra | unpublished radio broadcast of performance at sdr funkball |

rosen aus dem süden, waltz

| stuttgart 10 june 1983 | sdr orchestra | unpublished radio broadcast of performance at sdr funkball |

tritsch-tratsch polka

| stuttgart 22 june 1976 | sdr orchestra | unpublished radio broadcast |
| stuttgart 27 may 1981 | sdr orchestra | unpublished radio broadcast of performance at sdr funkball |

unter donner und blitz, polka

stuttgart 9 june 1982	sdr orchestra	unpublished radio broadcast of performance at sdr funkball

wiener blut, waltz

milan 22 february 1960	rai milano orchestra	lp: cetra LAR 22 cd: nuova era NE 2291/NE 2393-2398
stuttgart 9 june 1982	sdr orchestra	unpublished radio broadcast of performance at sdr funkball

der zigeunerbaron, einzugsmarsch

stuttgart 10 june 1983	sdr orchestra	unpublished radio broadcast of performance at sdr funkball

RICHARD STRAUSS (1864-1949)

don juan

stuttgart 22 june 1976	sdr orchestra	cd: dg awaiting publication already issued in japan by galileo
chicago 16 april 1986	munich po	cd: concert artists' recordings FED 068
munich 18 october 1989	munich po	cd: meteor (japan) MCD 047
bucharest 14-16 february 1990	munich po	unpublished video recording of extracts from performance and rehearsal
tokyo 12 october 1990	munich po	cd: gewandhaus music circle (japan) CG 14

don quixote

milan 11 april 1968	rai milano orchestra tosalti	cd: arkadia CD 570/CDHP 570

feierlicher einzug der ritter des johanniterordens

munich 10 november 1985	munich po	unpublished video recording

ein heldenleben

stuttgart 8 november 1979	sdr orchestra	cd: dg awaiting publication already issued in japan by galileo and drum can

4 letzte lieder

rome 12 april 1969	rai roma orchestra janowitz	cd: arkadia CD 570/CDHP 570 cd: cetra CDAR 2012/CDO 136 cd: nuova era NE 2217/NE 2393-2398
munich november 1992	munich po norman	cd: concert artists' recordings FED 027

till eulenspiegels lustige streiche

stuttgart 7 january 1965	sdr orchestra	cd: arkadia 487/CDMP 487 cd: nuova era NE 2217/NE 2393-2398 vhs video: teldec 4509 957103 also issued in japan by galileo and green hill; teldec and green hill also include rehearsal extracts

tod und verklärung

turin 30 april 1970	rai torino orchestra	cd: cetra CDAR 2012/CDO 136 cd: arkadia CD 487/CDMP 487 cd: nuova era NE 2217/NE 2393-2398 nuova era dated 1969
stuttgart 23 november 1972	sdr orchestra	unpublished radio broadcast
stuttgart 11 november 1982	sdr orchestra	cd: dg awaiting publication already issued in japan by galileo and meteor
munich date not confirmed	munich po	cd: audior (japan) AUDSE 504

IGOR STRAVINSKY (1882-1971)

le baiser de la fée

stuttgart 22 october 1964	sdr orchestra	unpublished radio broadcast
stuttgart 29 november 1974 and 12 march 1976	sdr orchestra	cd: andromeda NAS 2501 cd: arlecchino ARLA 82 cd: originals SH 803 cd: dg awaiting publication

jeu de cartes

berlin february- march 1950	bpo	lp: cetra LO 533 cd: nuova era NE 2301-2302

l'oiseau de feu, ballet suite

stuttgart 1967	sdr orchestra	unpublished video recording of excerpts
turin 17 october 1969	rai torino orchestra	cd: cetra CDAR 2008/CDO 136
tübingen 23 march 1978	sdr orchestra	unpublished radio broadcast
stuttgart 24 november 1978	sdr orchestra	cd: exclusive EX93T 66 cd: arlecchino ARLA 82 cd: dg awaiting publication

3 movements from petruhka

wiesbaden 23 march 1974	sdr orchestra	unpublished radio broadcast

suite no 2 for small orchestra

stuttgart 11 september 1958	sdr orchestra	unpublished radio broadcast

symphony of psalms

paris 23 december 1973	orchestre national and chorus	cd: exclusive EX93T 66 cd: arlecchino ARLA 82
stuttgart 5 april 1974	sdr orchestra and chorus	unpublished radio broadcast

PIOTR TCHAIKOVSKY (1840-1893)

symphony no 2 "little russian"

berlin 21 february 1950	bpo	lp: cetra LO 533 cd: arkadia CD 734/CDGI 734 cd: nuova era NE 2301-2302

symphony no 4

munich 30 september 1988	munich po	cd: concert artists' recordings FED 022-023

symphony no 5

london 5-9 july 1948	lpo	78: decca AK 2036-2041 78: london (usa) LA 136 lp: decca LXT 2545/ECM 833 lp: london (usa) LLP 168 cd: decca 425 9582 cd: grammofono AB 78837
stuttgart 23 february 1980	sdr orchestra	cd: meteor (japan) MCD 049
munich 16 january 1982	munich po	cd: concert artists' recordings FED 022-023
munich 29 may 1991	munich po	cd: emi CDC 556 5222/CDS 556 5172
bremen 10 june 1993	munich po	cd: audior (japan) AUDSE 522 also issued in japan by topazio

symphony no 6 "pathétique"

cologne 21 october 1957	wdr orchestra	lp: replica RPL 2466
stuttgart 17 september 1959	sdr orchestra	unpublished radio broadcast
milan 22 january 1960	rai milano orchestra	lp: rococo 2138 lp: melodram MEL 217 lp: movimento musica 01.006 lp: cetra LAR 5 cd: cetra CDAR 2061 cd: arkadia CD 402/CDMP 402
stuttgart 10 december 1976	sdr orchestra	unpublished radio broadcast
munich 1980	munich po	cd: meteor (japan) MCD 022
munich 14 november 1992	munich po	cd: emi CDC 556 5232/CDS 556 5172
tokyo 28 april 1993	munich po	cd: gewandhaus music circle (japan) CG 15

piano concerto no 1

ingolstadt 16 september 1989	munich po barenboim	cd: concert artists' recordings FED 022-023 also unpublished video recording
munich october 1991	munich po barenboim	vhs video: teldec 4509 941923

romeo and juliet

turin 4 april 1960	rai torino orchestra	lp: cetra LAR 10 cd: cetra CDAR 2013/CDAR 2061 cd: arkadia CD 402/CDMP 402 cd: nuova era NE 6327/NE 2393-2398
stuttgart 19 november 1976	sdr orchestra	cd: meteor (japan) MCD 026 also issued in japan by kyoung
munich january 1992	munich po	cd: emi CDC 556 5292

casse noisette, ballet suite

london 28-29 december 1948 and 22 july 1949	lpo	78: decca AK 2148-2150 78: london (usa) LA 86 lp: decca ECM 836 lp: london (usa) LPS 117 cd: decca 425 9582 cd: grammofono AB 78837
lugano 14 june 1963	swiss-italian radio orchestra	cd: ermitage ERM 114/120 032 excerpts cd: live classic best (japan) LCB 024/LCB 112
munich 10 february 1991	munich po	cd: audior (japan) AUDSE 505 also issued in japan by partita

valse des fleurs/casse noisette

milan 22 february 1960	rai milano orchestra	lp: cetra LAR 22 cd: nuova era NE 2291/NE 2393-2398
stuttgart 9 june 1982	sdr orchestra	unpublished radio broadcast of performance at sdr funkball

capriccio italien

stuttgart 5 june 1965	sdr orchestra	unpublished radio broadcast

francesca da rimini

stuttgart 11 april 1975	sdr orchestra	unpublished radio broadcast

GIUSEPPE VERDI (1813-1901)

la forza del destino, overture

milan date not confirmed	rai milano orchestra	cd: originals SH 841
stuttgart 11 february 1977	sdr orchestra	unpublished radio broadcast
bucharest 14-16 february 1990	munich po	cd: kyoun (japan) SCD 629-630 vhs video: teldec 4509 964383 rehearsal performance

ANTONIO VIVALDI (1678-1741)

violin concerto in d

berlin 9 november 1953	bpo heller	cd: arkadia CD 734/CDGI 734

minuet/concerto in f

milan 22 february 1960	rai milano orchestra	lp: cetra LAR 22

stabat mater

naples 5 january 1959	rai napoli orchestra and chorus höffgen	cd: arkadia CD 425/CDMP 425

RICHARD WAGNER (1813-1883)

götterdämmerung, siegfried's funeral march

munich 3-4 february 1993	munich po	cd: emi CDC 556 5242/CDS 556 5172

die meistersinger von nürnberg, overture

munich 6 december 1983	munich po	cd: concert artists' recordings FED 026
munich 10 november 1985	munich po	unpublished video recording
munich 3-4 february 1993	munich po	cd: emi CDC 556 5242/CDS 556 5172

parsifal, good friday music

munich 6 december 1983	munich po	cd: concert artists' recordings FED 026

siegfried idyll

| milan
20 november
1960 | rai milano
orchestra | cd: arkadia CD 750/CDGI 750 |
| munich
3-4
february
1993 | munich po | cd: emi CDC 556 5242/CDS 556 5172 |

tannhäuser, overture

| munich
6 december
1983 | munich po | cd: concert artists' recordings FED 026 |
| munich
3-4
february
1993 | munich po | cd: emi CDC 556 5242/CDS 556 5172 |

tristan und isolde, prelude and liebestod

stuttgart 22 november 1966	sdr orchestra	lp: rococo 2139 cd: arkadia CD 750/CDGI 750
stuttgart 8 march 1974	sdr orchestra	lp: rococo 2139 cd: arkadia CD 750/CDGI 750 <u>incorrectly dated 22 november 1966</u>
munich 6 december 1983	munich po	cd: concert artists' recordings FED 026 <u>also issued in japan by meteor</u>

wesendonk-lieder

munich 6 december 1983	munich po baniewicz	cd: concert artists' recordings FED 050

CARL MARIA VON WEBER (1786-1826)

euryanthe, overture

stuttgart 23 november 1972	sdr orchestra	unpublished radio broadcast

der freischütz, overture

stuttgart 17 october 1978	sdr orchestra	cd: kyoun (japan) SCD 629-630

oberon, overture

stuttgart 28 february 1982	sdr orchestra	cd: exclusive EX92T 37-38 cd: arlecchino ARLA 95 also issued in japan by meteor; arlecchino dated 1979
munich date not confirmed	munich po	cd: audior (japan) AUDSE 520-521 also issued in japan by topazio

HUGO WOLF (1860-1903)

italian serenade

rome 11 may 1968	rai roma orchestra	cd: arkadia CD 763/CDGI 763

THE LONDON SYMPHONY ORCHESTRA

Founded 1904
Patron: Her Majesty The Queen
President: Karl Böhm
Principal Conductor: Claudio Abbado
Principal Guest Conductors: Sir Colin Davis, C.B.E., Yevgeny Svetlanov
Conductor Emeritus: André Previn
Leader: Michael Davis

JOHANNES BRAHMS
(1833–1897)
EIN DEUTSCHES REQUIEM

THERE WILL BE NO INTERVAL DURING THIS PERFORMANCE

ISOBEL BUCHANAN
Soprano

ALAN TITUS
Baritone

LONDON SYMPHONY CHORUS
Director Richard Hickox

SERGIU CELIBIDACHE
Conductor

Thursday 16th April 1981 at 8.00
Sunday 19th April 1981 at 7.30
Sponsored by British Airways

Programme Book 45p

Greater London Council   South Bank Concert Halls
Royal Festival Hall   General Manager Michael Kaye

THIRTY YEARS
OF GREAT MUSIC

ROYAL ALBERT HALL

(Manager : C. S. Taylor)

LONDON PHILHARMONIC ORCHESTRA

Conductor :

CELIBIDACHE

Sunday, December 26th, 1948 at 7 p.m.

Smoking is not permitted in the auditorium.

Programme Sixpence

PROGRAMME

Overture, Hansel and Gretel - - Humperdinck

Pastoral Symphony (*Messiah*) - - Handel

Classical Symphony - - - Prokofiev
Allegro con brio
Larghetto
Gavotte : *Non troppo allegro*
Finale : *Molto vivace*

Four Dances from the Ballet "Gayaneh" - Khachaturyan
(*a*) *Dance of the Young Maidens*
(*b*) *Lullaby*
(*c*) *Lezghinka*
(*d*) *Sabre Dance*

INTERVAL

Symphony No. 5 in E minor - - Tchaikovsky
Andante – Allegro con anima
Andante cantabile, con alcuna licenza
Valse: *Allegro moderato*
Andante maestoso—Allegro vivace

Conductor : CELIBIDACHE

The London Philharmonic Orchestra is in association
with the Arts Council of Great Britain

The London Symphony Orchestra

Founded 1904	*Principal Conductor*	*Guest Leader*
	André Previn	Raymond Cohen
Patron		
Her Majesty The Queen	*Principal Guest*	
	Conductors	
President	Claudio Abbado	
Karl Böhm	Colin Davis	

Thursday 19 April at 8pm

Greater London Council
Royal Festival Hall
Director: George Mann OBE

Programme Book 30p

Strauss
Till Eulenspiegel

Kodaly
Dances from Galanta

Interval

Dvorak
Symphony No. 7, in D minor, Op. 70

Sergiu Celibidache
Conductor

A Peter Stuyvesant Concert

The London Symphony Orchestra

Founded 1904

Patron
Her Majesty The Queen

President
Karl Böhm

Principal Conductor
André Previn

*Principal Guest
Conductors*
Claudio Abbado
Colin Davis

Conductor
Eugen Jocl

Leader
John Geor

Thursday 6 April at 8pm

Greater London Council
Royal Festival Hall
Director: George Mann OBE

Programme Book 30p

Stravinsky
Three Dances from 'Petrusl

Debussy
Ibéria

Interval

Brahms
Symphony No. 4 in E minor

Sergiu Celibidache
Conductor

a
RANK XEROX
concert

Sergiu Celibidache's visit to England, and
forthcoming Spanish tour with him, have b
in association with Harold Holt Ltd., and I

THE LONDON SYMPHONY ORCHESTRA

Founded 1904
Patron: **Her Majesty The Queen**
President: **Karl Böhm**
Principal Conductor: **André Previn**
Principal Guest Conductors: **Claudio Abbado, Colin Davis**
Guest Leader: **Hugh Maguire**

Sergiu Celibidache conductor

We are very grateful to Maestro Celibidache for kindly agreeing to conduct
this concert in place of Dr. Karl Böhm, who is indisposed

Brahms

Symphony No. 3 in F major, Op. 90

Interval

Symphony No. 1 in C minor, Op. 68

Thursday 31 May at 8pm

Greater London Council
Royal Festival Hall
Director: George Mann OBE

Programme Book 35p

65th Annual Series of Concerts. This concert is presented by the London Symphony
Orchestra Limited with financial support from the London Orchestral Concert Board
(representing the Arts Council of Great Britain and the Greater London Council).

A **British airways** Concert

A **British airways** Concert

Concert Season 1978/9

The London Symphony Orchestra

Founded 1904

Patron
Her Majesty The Queen

President
Karl Böhm

Principal Conductor
André Previn

Principal Guest Conductors
Claudio Abbado
Colin Davis

Conductor Laureate
Eugen Jochum

Leader
John Georgiadis

Tuesday 11 April at 8pm

Greater London Council
Royal Festival Hall
Director: George Mann OBE

Programme Book 30p

Verdi
Overture, La Forza del Destino

Hindemith
Mathis der Maler Symphony

Interval

Prokofiev
Romeo and Juliet Suite

Sergiu Celibidache
Conductor

a
British airways
Concert

Sergiu Celibidache's visit to England, and the LSO's
forthcoming Spanish tour with him, have been arranged
in association with Harold Holt Ltd., and Ibermusica SA.

Credits

Valuable help with the supply of
information or illustration material
came from

Kenzo Amoh　　　　Richard Chlupaty
Siam Chowkwayun　Paul Geffen
Michael Gray　　　　Syd Gray
Bill Holland　　　　Ken Jagger
Bruce Morrison　　Alan Newcombe
Tatsuro Ouchi　　　Brian Pinder
Ulf Scharlau　　　　Hisashi Takei
Ates Tanin　　　　　Peter Taylor
Malcolm Walker　　Urs Weber

Music and Books published by Travis & Emery Music Bookshop:

Anon.: Hymnarium Sarisburiense, cum Rubricis et Notis Musicis.
Agricola, Johann Friedrich from Tosi: Anleitung zur Singkunst.
Bach, C.P.E.: edited W. Emery: Nekrolog or Obituary Notice of J.S. Bach.
Bateson, Naomi Judith: Alcock of Salisbury
Bathe, William: A Briefe Introduction to the Skill of Song (c.1587)
Bax, Arnold: Symphony #5, Arranged for Piano Four Hands by Walter Emery
Burney, Charles: The Present State of Music in France and Italy (1771)
Burney, Charles: The Present State of Music in Germany, Netherlands... (1773)
Burney, Charles: An Account of the Musical Performances ... Handel (1784)
Burney, Karl: Nachricht von Georg Friedrich Handel's Lebensumstanden (1784)
Burns, Robert: The Caledonian Musical Museum ... Best Scotch Songs (1810)
Cobbett, W.W.: Cobbett's Cyclopedic Survey of Chamber Music. (2 vols.)
Corrette, Michel: Le Maitre de Clavecin (1753)
Crimp, Bryan: Dear Mr. Rosenthal … Dear Mr. Gaisberg …
Crimp, Bryan: Solo: The Biography of Solomon
d'Indy, Vincent: Beethoven: Biographie Critique (in French, 1911)
d'Indy, Vincent: Beethoven: A Critical Biography (in English, 1912)
d'Indy, Vincent: César Franck (in French, 1910)
Fischhof, Joseph: Versuch einer Geschichte des Clavierbaues (1853).
Frescobaldi, Girolamo: D'Arie Musicali per Cantarsi. Primo & Secondo Libro.
Geminiani, Francesco: The Art of Playing the Violin (1751)
Handel; Purcell; Boyce et al: Calliope or English Harmony: Vol. First. (1746)
Häuser: Musikalisches Lexikon. 2 vols in one.
Hawkins, John: General History of the Science & Practice of Music (5 vols. 1776)
Herbert-Caesari, Edgar: The Science and Sensations of Vocal Tone
Herbert-Caesari, Edgar: Vocal Truth
Hopkins and Rimboult: The Organ. Its History and Construction.
Hunt, John: Adam to Webern: the recordings of von Karajan
Hunt, John: several discographies – see separate list.
Isaacs, Lewis: Hänsel and Gretel. A Guide to Humperdinck's Opera.
Isaacs, Lewis: Königskinder (Royal Children) A Guide to Humperdinck's Opera.
Kastner: Manuel Général de Musique Militaire
Lacassagne, M. l'Abbé Joseph : Traité Général des élémens du Chant.
Lascelles (née Catley), Anne: The Life of Miss Anne Catley.
Mainwaring, John: Memoirs of the Life of the Late George Frederic Handel
Malcolm, Alexander: A Treaty of Music: Speculative, Practical and Historical
Marx, Adolph Bernhard: Die Kunst des Gesanges, Theoretisch-Practisch (1826)
May, Florence: The Life of Brahms (2nd edition)
May, Florence: The Girlhood Of Clara Schumann: Clara Wieck And Her Time.
Mellers, Wilfrid: Angels of the Night: Popular Female Singers of Our Time
Mellers, Wilfrid: Bach and the Dance of God
Mellers, Wilfrid: Beethoven and the Voice of God
Mellers, Wilfrid: Caliban Reborn - Renewal in Twentieth Century Music

Music and Books published by Travis & Emery Music Bookshop:

Mellers, Wilfrid: François Couperin and the French Classical Tradition
Mellers, Wilfrid: Harmonious Meeting
Mellers, Wilfrid: Le Jardin Retrouvé, The Music of Frederic Mompou
Mellers, Wilfrid: Music and Society, England and the European Tradition
Mellers, Wilfrid: Music in a New Found Land: ... ... American Music
Mellers, Wilfrid: Romanticism and the Twentieth Century (from 1800)
Mellers, Wilfrid: The Masks of Orpheus: ...... the Story of European Music.
Mellers, Wilfrid: The Sonata Principle (from c. 1750)
Mellers, Wilfrid: Vaughan Williams and the Vision of Albion
Panchianio, Cattuffio: Rutzvanscad Il Giovine (1737)
Pearce, Charles: Sims Reeves, Fifty Years of Music in England.
Pettitt, Stephen: Philharmonia Orchestra: Complete Discography (1987)
Playford, John: An Introduction to the Skill of Musick (1674)
Purcell, Henry et al: Harmonia Sacra ... The First Book, (1726)
Purcell, Henry et al: Harmonia Sacra ... Book II (1726)
Quantz, Johann: Versuch einer Anweisung die Flöte traversiere zu spielen.
Rameau, Jean-Philippe: Code de Musique Pratique, ou Methodes (1760)
Rastall, Richard: The Notation of Western Music.
Rimbault, Edward: The Pianoforte, Its Origins, Progress, and Construction.
Rousseau, Jean Jacques: Dictionnaire de Musique
Rubinstein, Anton : Guide to the proper use of the Pianoforte Pedals.
Sainsbury, John S.: Dictionary of Musicians. Vol. 1. (1825). 2 vols.
Serré de Rieux, Jean de : Les dons des Enfans de Latone
Simpson, Christopher: A Compendium of Practical Musick in Five Parts
Spohr, Louis: Autobiography
Spohr, Louis: Grand Violin School
Tans'ur, William: A New Musical Grammar; or The Harmonical Spectator
Terry, Charles Sanford: John Christian Bach (Johann Christian Bach) (1929)
Terry, Charles Sanford: J.S. Bach's Original Hymn-Tunes for Congregational Use
Terry, Charles Sanford: Four-Part Chorals of J.S. Bach. (German & English)
Terry, Charles Sanford: Joh. Seb. Bach, Cantata Texts, Sacred and Secular.
Terry, Charles Sanford: The Origins of the Family of Bach Musicians.
Tosi, Pierfrancesco: Opinioni de' Cantori Antichi, e Moderni (1723)
Van der Straeten, Edmund: History of the Violoncello, The Viol da Gamba ...
Van der Straeten, Edmund: History of the Violin, Its Ancestors... (2 vols.)
Waltern: Musikalisches Lexicon
Walther, J. G.: Musicalisches Lexikon ober Musicalische Bibliothec

Travis & Emery Music Bookshop
17 Cecil Court, London, WC2N 4EZ, United Kingdom.
Tel. (+44) 20 7240 2129

© Travis & Emery 2009

Discographies by Travis & Emery:

Discographies by John Hunt.

1987: 978-1-906857-14-1: From Adam to Webern: the Recordings of von Karajan.

1991: 978-0-951026-83-0: 3 Italian Conductors and 7 Viennese Sopranos: 10 Discographies: Arturo Toscanini, Guido Cantelli, Carlo Maria Giulini, Elisabeth Schwarzkopf, Irmgard Seefried, Elisabeth Gruemmer, Sena Jurinac, Hilde Gueden, Lisa Della Casa, Rita Streich.

1992: 978-0-951026-85-4: Mid-Century Conductors and More Viennese Singers: 10 Discographies: Karl Boehm, Victor De Sabata, Hans Knappertsbusch, Tullio Serafin, Clemens Krauss, Anton Dermota, Leonie Rysanek, Eberhard Waechter, Maria Reining, Erich Kunz.

1993: 978-0-951026-87-8: More 20th Century Conductors: 7 Discographies: Eugen Jochum, Ferenc Fricsay, Carl Schuricht, Felix Weingartner, Josef Krips, Otto Klemperer, Erich Kleiber.

1994: 978-0-951026-88-5: Giants of the Keyboard: 6 Discographies: Wilhelm Kempff, Walter Gieseking, Edwin Fischer, Clara Haskil, Wilhelm Backhaus, Artur Schnabel.

1994: 978-0-951026-89-2: Six Wagnerian Sopranos: 6 Discographies: Frieda Leider, Kirsten Flagstad, Astrid Varnay, Martha Moedl, Birgit Nilsson, Gwyneth Jones.

1995: 978-0-952582-70-0: Musical Knights: 6 Discographies: Henry Wood, Thomas Beecham, Adrian Boult, John Barbirolli, Reginald Goodall, Malcolm Sargent.

1995: 978-0-952582-71-7: A Notable Quartet: 4 Discographies: Gundula Janowitz, Christa Ludwig, Nicolai Gedda, Dietrich Fischer-Dieskau.

1996: 978-0-952582-72-4: The Post-War German Tradition: 5 Discographies: Rudolf Kempe, Joseph Keilberth, Wolfgang Sawallisch, Rafael Kubelik, Andre Cluytens.

1996: 978-0-952582-73-1: Teachers and Pupils: 7 Discographies: Elisabeth Schwarzkopf, Maria Ivoguen, Maria Cebotari, Meta Seinemeyer, Ljuba Welitsch, Rita Streich, Erna Berger.

1996: 978-0-952582-77-9: Tenors in a Lyric Tradition: 3 Discographies: Peter Anders, Walther Ludwig, Fritz Wunderlich.

1997: 978-0-952582-78-6: The Lyric Baritone: 5 Discographies: Hans Reinmar, Gerhard Huesch, Josef Metternich, Hermann Uhde, Eberhard Waechter.

1997: 978-0-952582-79-3: Hungarians in Exile: 3 Discographies: Fritz Reiner, Antal Dorati, George Szell.

1997: 978-1-901395-00-6: The Art of the Diva: 3 Discographies: Claudia Muzio, Maria Callas, Magda Olivero.

1997: 978-1-901395-01-3: Metropolitan Sopranos: 4 Discographies: Rosa Ponselle, Eleanor Steber, Zinka Milanov, Leontyne Price.

1997: 978-1-901395-02-0: Back From The Shadows: 4 Discographies: Willem Mengelberg, Dimitri Mitropoulos, Hermann Abendroth, Eduard Van Beinum.

1997: 978-1-901395-03-7: More Musical Knights: 4 Discographies: Hamilton Harty, Charles Mackerras, Simon Rattle, John Pritchard.

1998: 978-1-901395-94-5: Conductors On The Yellow Label: 8 Discographies: Fritz Lehmann, Ferdinand Leitner, Ferenc Fricsay, Eugen Jochum, Leopold Ludwig, Artur Rother, Franz Konwitschny, Igor Markevitch.

1998: 978-1-901395-95-2: More Giants of the Keyboard: 5 Discographies: Claudio Arrau, Gyorgy Cziffra, Vladimir Horowitz, Dinu Lipatti, Artur Rubinstein.

1998: 978-1-901395-96-9: Mezzo and Contraltos: 5 Discographies: Janet Baker, Margarete Klose, Kathleen Ferrier, Giulietta Simionato, Elisabeth Hoengen.

1999: 978-1-901395-97-6: The Furtwaengler Sound Sixth Edition: Discography and
Concert Listing.
1999: 978-1-901395-98-3: The Great Dictators: 3 Discographies: Evgeny Mravinsky,
Artur Rodzinski, Sergiu Celibidache.
1999: 978-1-901395-99-0: Sviatoslav Richter: Pianist of the Century: Discography.
2000: 978-1-901395-04-4: Philharmonic Autocrat 1: Discography of: Herbert Von
Karajan [Third Edition].
2000: 978-1-901395-05-1: Wiener Philharmoniker 1 - Vienna Philharmonic and
Vienna State Opera Orchestras: Discography Part 1 1905-1954.
2000: 978-1-901395-06-8: Wiener Philharmoniker 2 - Vienna Philharmonic and
Vienna State Opera Orchestras: Discography Part 2 1954-1989.
2001: 978-1-901395-07-5: Gramophone Stalwarts: 3 Separate Discographies: Bruno
Walter, Erich Leinsdorf, Georg Solti.
2001: 978-1-901395-08-2: Singers of the Third Reich: 5 Discographies: Helge
Roswaenge, Tiana Lemnitz, Franz Voelker, Maria Mueller, Max Lorenz.
2001: 978-1-901395-09-9: Philharmonic Autocrat 2: Concert Register of Herbert Von
Karajan Second Edition.
2002: 978-1-901395-10-5: Sächsische Staatskapelle Dresden: Complete Discography.
2002: 978-1-901395-11-2: Carlo Maria Giulini: Discography and Concert Register.
2002: 978-1-901395-12-9: Pianists For The Connoisseur: 6 Discographies: Arturo
Benedetti Michelangeli, Alfred Cortot, Alexis Weissenberg, Clifford Curzon,
Solomon, Elly Ney.
2003: 978-1-901395-14-3: Singers on the Yellow Label: 7 Discographies: Maria
Stader, Elfriede Troetschel, Annelies Kupper, Wolfgang Windgassen, Ernst
Haefliger, Josef Greindl, Kim Borg.
2003: 978-1-901395-15-0: A Gallic Trio: 3 Discographies: Charles Muench, Paul
Paray, Pierre Monteux.
2004: 978-1-901395-16-7: Antal Dorati 1906-1988: Discography and Concert
Register.
2004: 978-1-901395-17-4: Columbia 33CX Label Discography.
2004: 978-1-901395-18-1: Great Violinists: 3 Discographies: David Oistrakh,
Wolfgang Schneiderhan, Arthur Grumiaux.
2006: 978-1-901395-19-8: Leopold Stokowski: Second Edition of the Discography.
2006: 978-1-901395-20-4: Wagner Im Festspielhaus: Discography of the Bayreuth
Festival.
2006: 978-1-901395-21-1: Her Master's Voice: Concert Register and Discography of
.Dame Elisabeth Schwarzkopf [Third Edition].
2007: 978-1-901395-22-8: Hans Knappertsbusch: Kna: Concert Register and
Discography of Hans Knappertsbusch, 1888-1965. Second Edition.
2008: 978-1-901395-23-5: Philips Minigroove: Second Extended Version of the
European Discography.
2009: 978-1-901395--24-2: American Classics: The Discographies of Leonard
Bernstein and Eugene Ormandy.

Discography by Stephen J. Pettitt, edited by John Hunt:
1987: 978-1-906857-16-5: Philharmonia Orchestra: Complete Discography 1945-1987

Available from: Travis & Emery at 17 Cecil Court, London, UK.
(+44) 20 7 240 2129. email on sales@travis-and-emery.com .

9 781901 395983

Printed by BoD™in Norderstedt, Germany